100 Cultural Symbols of
Korea

100 windows showcasing Korea

Discovery media

100 Cultural Symbols of Korea

Foreword

100 Cultural Symbols of Korea

100 Windows Showcasing Korea

Metaphorically speaking, this book can be regarded as 100 individual windows into the past and present of Korea. Korea boasts a history that spans some 5,000 years. Over this long period of time, Koreans have created their own language, writing system, arts, culture, foods, and spiritual world. In this regard, the 100 windows introduced herein provide readers with an opportunity to find out who Koreans were and are, what they eat, and what kinds of thoughts have animated them during this long process. Furthermore, this book also offers readers insight into how modern-day Koreans live.

The first window opens to reveal the Korean national flag, or Taegeukgi. The information provided about the Taegeukgi in this window, such as the fact that it is based on the principles of the universe as studied and interpreted by Koreans, will lead readers to the conclusion that Korea is a country with a deep philosophical foundation.

A look inside the 21st window will allow readers to become immersed in the wonderful world of Korean IT.

While IT has generally been understood to refer to advanced technologies and science, the term has come to mean so much more in Korea. IT encompassed various elements that range from culture and everyday life to politics and art. It is at once a path to communication and a cyber agora in which discussions and debates can be carried out. Koreans have used this IT to create a completely new world the likes of which mankind has never experienced before.

The 27th window sheds some much needed light on a person who lived 5,000 years ago. Koreans, Korean history and Korean culture would not exist if it were not for this man known as Dangun the father of the Korean nation. As mentioned above, Korea boasts its own unique language and writing system. In this regard, linguists the world over have praised Hangeul as the most scientific and systematic writing system ever created, and as one of the most advanced types of languages. This book allows readers to encounter not only this astounding writing system known as Hangeul, but also the person who created it. Surprisingly, the person who created Hangeul was a king, not a linguist. This monarch has been regarded as the most intelligent, humane, and artistic king in Korean history. Readers can come face to face with this man (King Sejong) in the 30th window and with his creation (Hangeul) in the 82nd.

The 100th and final window opens to reveal the Korean love story known as the *Chunhyangjeon*. The story of Chunhyang is a beautiful and yet sad Korean tale of love that can be compared to that of Romeo and Juliet. This book also includes many other windows that introduce unique aspects of Korea. For instance, readers can encounter and experience Korea's stunning nature, inimitable cities, traditional food and folklore, and the profound religions and aesthetic arts that have developed on the peninsula.

This work would not have been possible without the help of many wonderful people. We would like to begin by thanking You Young-Ki and Michael Bujold for their wonderful rendering of the original Korean draft into English. We would like to thank Korean traditional cuisine researcher and food coordinator Kim Young-hee for her loving preparation of the Korean dishes introduced in these pages and fashion designer Lee Young-hee for her outstanding photographs. Special thanks also goes out to photographer Gwon Tae-gyun, seal-engraving artist Jeong Byeong-rye, photographer Kim Gwan-jung, artist Lee Jong-song, and photographer Baek Ji-soon. We would also like to single out the National Museum of Korea, Kyujanggak Institute for Korean Studies, Provincial Government of Jeju, and the Hyundai Asan Corporation for their invaluable assistance. Last, but certainly not least, we would like to offer our heartfelt thanks to the Korea Foundation for its provision of the funds needed to publish this book.

Authors Yoo Myeong-jong, Lee Ji-hye
Photographer Jeon Sung-young

Chapter 01

National Symbols

Taegeukgi / Mugunghwa

Taegeukgi: The National Flag of Korea

The term taegeuk literally means the "state of chaos that existed before the creation of the sky and earth." In this regard, while the red portion of the taegeuk symbol signifies yang, the blue section is meant to denote yin. This yin and yang can in turn be expressed as the moon and sun, or earth and heaven. Taegeuk thus has been taken to mean a complete circle in which yin and yang encounter one another, or an unlimited universe. Taegeuk is therefore a different term for the universe.

To this end, taegeuk designs were first found in conjunction with ruins and remains from the 7th century. One can find many taegeuk designs in pagodas, roof tiles, knives, sculptures, gates, and fans. This highly symbolical design was subsequently reborn as the taegukgi during the modern era. In 1876 King Gojong (reign 1864 - 1907) of Joseon Dynasty (1392 - 1910) personally designed a taegeukgi (Korean national flag) which prominently featured the taegeuk. This flag was first officially used to represent Korea in 1882 when a royal envoy visiting Japan hung it from the roof of the building where his delegation was staying.

Originally known as the 'Joseon gukgi (flag of Joseon)', the Korean flag was first referred to as the taegeukgi in the March 1st, 1919 Declaration of Korean Independence signed by 33 national representatives during the Japanese colonial era. The people who subsequently poured out onto the streets to participate in the spontaneous independence movement did so while holding such taegeukgi in their hands. In 1949, the newly established Korean government set clear norms in terms of the size and form which the taegeukgi was to have, standards which continue to apply to this day.

The 2002 Korea-Japan World Cup had the effect of forever altering Koreans' perception of the taegeukgi. During this magical period, the taegeukgi came to be seen as more than an object that should be saluted on national holidays and special occasions. Adorned on people's faces, t-shirts, towels and cloaks, it effectively became one of the items people used to express their support for the national side. The taegeukgi has thus become perceived as a more intimate part of the people's daily lives.

Mugunghwa: The national flower of Korea

The bellowing and unassuming Mugunghwa (rose of Sharon) is the national flower of Korea. While it boasts neither an extravagant appearance nor strong aroma, this plain-looking flower is embedded with a never-ending sense of vitality that meshes seamlessly with the unswerving Korean national character. The mugunghwa embodies such notions as devotion, gentleness, and endurance.

The mugunghwa has been with Koreans since time long past. In a record of the history of Gojoseon (2333 BC-108 BC) known as the *Handangoki*, one encounters a flower called the hwanhwa. Here, this hwanhwa can be understood to denote none other than the mugunghwa, which has also been referred to at other times as the mokkeun or geunhwa.

A diplomatic document sent from Silla Kingdom (57 BC - 935 AD) to China's Tang dynasty contained a reference to Silla as the land of the scent of Geunhwa (or country of mugunghwa). Moreover, the ancient Chinese geographic collection *ShanHaiJing* (Classic of the Mountains and Seas) and the *Gujinzhu* (encyclopedia) compiled during the Qin (221 BC - 206 AD) dynasty include references to Korea as the land of ample mugunghwa.

The actual term mugunghwa was first employed during the Goryeo Dynasty (918 - 1392). More to the point, the first reference to mugunghwa appears in the *Dongguk isanggukjip* (Collected Works of Minister Yi of Korea) written by the Goryeo Dynasty era scribe Yi Gyu-bo (1168 - 1241). During the Goryeo Dynasty and Joseon Dynasty eras (1392 - 1910), it was common practice for kings to reward those who successfully passed the civil service examinations (gwageo) with paper-made mugunghwa.

The mugunghwa first became the national flower of Korea during the Japanese colonial era (1910 - 1945) when it was overwhelmingly selected by the people as the floral symbol of their nation. Koreans countered colonial Japan's racial assimilation policy by planting mugunghwa nationwide as a sign of their uninterrupted dreams of independence for Korea. Therefore, the mugunghwa which regularly returns a day after seemingly having faded away to gloriously expose its existence, became a symbol of the unbridled and unbreakable spirit of the Korean nation. In modern times, the mugunghwa has become a signifier to demonstrate the identity of Koreans.

100 Cultural Symbols of Korea

Chapter 02

Nature, Science & technology

Dokdo: The Spiritual Island

Dokdo is a small volcanic island located at the eastern-most end of the Korean landmass. Dokdo, which spouted out of the East Sea some 4.6 million years ago, is the oldest of Korea's volcanic islands. While Dokdo was originally one island, erosion and inclement weather has over the years resulted in it becoming divided into Eastern and Western islands. While Eastern island (dongdo) stands 88 meters tall, Western island (seodo) rises 174 meters above the sea. Although it is a small island with an area of only 0.186 km2, Dokdo represents much more than a simple island for Koreans. Dokdo constitutes nothing less than the pride of Koreans.

Japan has often asserted that it has territorial sovereignty over Dokdo. However, nothing could be further from the truth. Japan illegally occupied Dokdo during the so-called colonial era (1910 - 1945) in which it usurped the sovereignty of Korea. In this regard, not only Korean historical records and atlases but several Japanese ones as well, have clearly included Dokdo as part of Korea's territory. For instance, the record of ancient Korean history known as the *Samguk sagi* , Chronicles of the Three Kingdoms, states that Dokdo first became a part of the Korean territory during the reign of King Jijeung of Silla Kingdom (512). At that time, an independent kingdom called Usanguk existed in the East Sea.

This Usanguk was composed of the island currently known as Ulleungdo and Dokdo. Usanguk was subsequently occupied and integrated into Silla Kingdom during the reign of King Jijeung. Meanwhile, the *Joseon wangjosillok* (Annals of Joseon Dynasty) - 472 years of historical records compiled from 1392 to 1863- also contains many records pertaining to Dokdo.

Moreover, the *Sinjeung dongguk yeoji seungnam* (Revised and Augmented Gazetteer of Korea), a book which introduced the geography of Joseon compiled in 1531,

also clearly reveals that Dokdo belongs to Korea. Finally, the ancient Japanese document, the *Onshu shicho goki* (Records on Observations in Oki Province) (compiled in 1667), also plainly places Dokdo within the boundaries of Korea.

The marine area around Dokdo has long been known as a golden fishing area. This is because its location as the meeting point between the cold currents that emanate from the north and the warm currents flowing from the south make it a natural home for copious amounts of plankton. There are currently a few civilians, marine guards, and the officer of lighthouse residing on Dokdo.

© Kim Kwan-jung

Baekdudaegan:
The Backbone of the Korean Peninsula

The term Baekdu daegan refers to an elongated mountain ridge that runs through the entire Korean peninsula, spanning from Baekdu Mountain in the north, to Jiri Mountain in the south. 1,400 kilometers in length, it is often referred to as the backbone of the Korean peninsula. Baekdusan Mountain (2,744m), which stands at the northern reaches of the baekdu daegan, is widely perceived as the father of all Korean mountains. It is also regarded by the Korean nation as its most sacred mountain, and has been worshipped as such since the Gojoseon era (2333 BC - 108 BC).

Koreans have long perceived mountains as a connected ridge rather than as a chain of separate peaks. The mountain range that originates from Baekdusan Mountain stretches all the way down to Jirisan Mountain at the southern end of the Korean peninsula. The great majority of famous mountains in Korea, including Geumgangsan, Seolaksan, Odaesan, Songnisan and Deokyusan Mountains are located within the span of the baekdu dagan. The baekdu daegan can be likened to the backbone of the Korean peninsula. Much like people's ribs extend outwards from their backbone, so do the mountains of Korea from the baekdu daegan. There are also numerous rivers, which like the mountains, originate from the ridges of the baekdu daegan. These subsequently flow into the waters that make up Korea's East, West, and South Seas.

During the Japanese colonial era (1910 - 1945), imperial Japan attempted to restructure Korean mountains in accordance with the concept of mountain ranges. The notion of mountain ranges that prevailed during the Japanese colonial era was one based on geological structures under the ground rather than topographical ones. When viewed from the standpoint of the Japanese notion of mountain ranges, Korean mountains appear to be inconsistent with their actual topographies. However, when viewed based on the notion of the baekdu daegan, the contours of these same mountains begin to resemble their actual topographies in an eerily precise manner. Baekdu daegan is a uniquely Korean geographic theory that is based on an understanding of the national territory as a giant organism resembling the human body.

The valleys of Baekdu Mountain. The elongated mountain ridge known as the Baekdu daegan that runs through the entire Korean peninsula has its origins in Baekdu Mountain.

Baekdusan: The Father of Korean Mountains

Mt. Horeb in the Sinai Peninsula became a symbol of the identity of the nomadic tribe of slaves which Moses led out of Egypt. Since Moses first received the Ten Commandments on its slopes, Mt. Horeb has been regarded in the West as the holiest of all mountains. To this end, Baekdusan Mountain(2750m) has occupied a similar position of predilection in the hearts of the inhabitants of the Korean peninsula and Manchuria.

The very first state to emerge on the Korean peninsula, Gojoseon, was an ethnic community whose very roots lay in Mt. Baekdusan. From that time onwards, Mt. Baekdusan has been regarded by the Korean nation as much more than a mere mountain. In fact, Koreans believe that Mt. Baekdusan constitutes the point of origin of the Korean nation, and the home of its spirit. Scores of Koreans have scaled the slopes of Mt. Baekdusan over the years in search of the origin of their proud nation. In this regard, the mountain's inherent sense of sacredness is surpassed only by its magnificent beauty.

References to Mt. Baekdusan first began to emerge in documents and records during the 2nd century. It subsequently appeared under various names in geographical documents and historical writings. The term Mt. Baekdusan literally means white-haired mountain. As the top of the mountain was covered with snow in every season other than summer, people began to refer to it as Baekdu (white haired). Mt. Baekdusan has also been referred to by other names containing such meanings as 'great', 'long', 'magnificent', and 'sacred'.

Mt. Baekdusan is a dormant volcano that was active as recently as 100 years ago. The mountain's present features were formed over a long period of time that began with the development of a huge crater caused by a great explosion that occurred some 550,000 years ago and continued up until the above-mentioned volcanic explosion of 100 years ago. The magma under the ground created a large and beautiful volcanic lake (2189m in height, 14km in width, 4.5km in diameter, and 384m in depth) which Koreans refer to as cheonji (heaven lake). This dark green lake has maintained many of its prehistoric features, to the point that one would naturally expect to see pterosaurs flying over its shores.

Mt. Baekdusan is home to many animals such as tigers, Asiatic black bears, wolves, and deer. It also provides a fertile breeding ground for medicinal roots and rare trees such as mountain ginseng and the Ganoderma lucidum (Yeongji mushroom). Mt. Baekdusan also features beautiful waterfalls, sulfurous hot springs, and lakes of various sizes. In 1980, UNESCO added Mt. Baekdusan to its list of World Heritage Sites.

Geumgangsan: Jewel of Korean Mountains

Mt. Geumgangsan (1638m) is the Eros of Korea. All those who encounter this attractive goddess can never forget its majestic grandeur. In this regard, Koreans have perceived Mt. Geumgangsan as their muse since well before the middle ages. Believing that they would be unable to contemplate the meaning of the beauty of nature without having set their eyes on this regal mountain, practically every poet and artist who lived during the Joseon dynasty (1392 - 1910) made a pilgrimage to Mt. Geumgangsan. While many authors and artists during this period extolled Mt. Geumgangsan using the most beautiful of sentences and paintings, it is Jeong Seon (1676 - 1759) who has widely come to be regarded as the artist which best epitomizes the essence of Mt. Geumgangsan. Jeong is responsible for creating the uniquely Oriental painting style known as Jingyeong landscape painting that emerged during the latter half of Joseon. Much like Picasso is said to have been raised by the sunlight of the Mediterranean, so was Jeong Seon by the colors and scenery of Mt. Geumgangsan. Jeong's works related to Mt. Geumgangsan are widely perceived by art history scholars as masterpieces representing the height of Korean art.

Located at the mid-eastern end of the Korean peninsula, Mt. Geumgangsan falls within what is now North Korea. The division of the Korean peninsula in 1950 resulted in the South Korean people finding themselves unable to visit this beloved mountain for the better part of 50 years. The 155-mile long barbed wire fence erected as part of the DMZ (demilitarized zone) separating the two Koreas proved to be an obstacle stronger than any other barrier. However, efforts on the part of the two Korean governments to achieve reconcilia-tion eventually resulted in the opening of a marine tourism route to Mt. Geumgangsan in 1998. The opening of an over-land route to Mt. Geumgangsan in 2003 saw the partial col-lapse of the barbed wire that had long stood as the symbol of the national division. These divisive barriers were further weakened by the peace overtures made by South Korean President and Nobel Laureate Kim Dae-jung and his succes-sor President Roh Moo-hyun, as well as by Korean' passion to visit Mt. Geumgangsan. As such, Mt. Geumgangsan pos-sesses a beauty that is capable of melting even the most stringent of ideologies and barbed wire.

Mt. Geumgangsan is separated into the Oegeumgang (out-er Geumgang), Naegeumgang (inner Geumgang), and Haegeumgang (sea Geumgang). In this regard, while the Oegeumgang possesses an ornate beauty, the Naegeum-gang boasts mountainous scenery of unrivalled exquisite-ness. Meanwhile, the Haegeumgang, which consists of beautiful lakes, pine trees, and fantastically-shaped rocks, is regarded as being nothing short of an earthly paradise.

In Buddhist scriptures, the term Geumgang literally means the utopian world. However, Geumgang also means dia-mond. It was in this vein that in 1894 the British writer Is-abella Bird Bishop referred to it in her travelogue as 'Dia-mond Mountain.'

©Hyundai Asan

Donghae: A Deep Blue Expanse

Koreans of yore believed that a yongwang (Dragon King) lived in the Donghae. They also believed that over the horizon of this vast blue expanse lay the mysterious palace of a god. In this regard, the Donghae has held a place of predilection in the hearts of Koreans surpassed only by Baekdusan Mountain. Donghae is the name given to the sea that lays to the east of the Korean peninsula. Connected to the Okhotsk Sea to the north, the Japanese archipelago to the east and the Pacific Ocean via the Daehan Strait to the south, the Donghae spans 1,700km from south to north, and 1,100km from east to west. While it has an average depth of 1,361m, it descends some 4,049 m at its deepest point.

The interior of the Donghae can rightfully be regarded as a showcase for lagoons. It is almost as if the gods installed these beautiful jewels in the interior to make up for their hasty, simple design of the eastern coast of the Korean peninsula. A lagoon is a body of comparatively salty or brackish water separated from the deeper sea by a shallow or exposed sandbank. Lagoons feature tremen-dous landscapes and are of great ecological value.

Unlike the Seohae (West Sea) and Namhae (South Sea), the Donghae does not feature a multitude of islands. In this regard, Ulleungdo and Dokdo are the only inhabited islands. Resembling a diamond affixed to a large-size plate, the beautiful volcanic island of Ulleungdo stands out majestically from the waters of the Donghae. Located 137 km east of the Korean mainland, some 9,200 people call this island with an area of 72km² home. Ulleungdo is the center of the Korean squid industry.

Up until 1986, fishermen regularly used to catch not only squid but also whales in the waters of the Donghae. In fact, whale hunting in the Donghae can be traced all the way back to the prehistoric era. To this end, a depiction of the whale hunt has been uncovered in a rock carving found in the Ulsan neighborhood of Daegongni. This rock carving depicting the features of fishermen struggling with whales constitutes a historical artifact that succinctly showcases the lifestyle of those who lived during the prehistoric era.

Daedong yeojido: The Great Map of Korea: A Virtual Geography Museum

For Koreans land has always represented more than just mere land. Since times long past, Koreans have regarded land as an organic body with a life of its own. Ancient maps of Korea not only point out the location of objects, but also artistic portrayals of Koreans' perception of land. Therefore, while Korean atlases provide territorial information, they can simultaneously be perceived as beautiful drawings representative of Korean plastic arts. Kim Jeong-ho(1804 - 1866) has widely been perceived as the greatest geographer in the history of Korea. To this end, Kim Jeong-ho's *Daedong yeojido* (the Great Map of Korea) (1861) is a large-scale atlas that stands 3.3m wide and 6.7m long. Featuring less writing whenever possible than traditional maps and descriptions marked with signs and emblems, the *Daedong yeojido* exhibits many of the characteristics of a modern map. Moreover, the *Daedong yeojido* can be regarded as the most exact and complete of the numerous ancient atlases manufactured using traditional techniques. The extensive amount of text involved makes this map a virtual geography museum rendered on paper. In this re-gard, the *Daedong yeojido* has been perceived as a great cultural legacy that encompasses the entire territory of Korea.

The *Daedong yeojido* is a woodcut map. One of the first things which catches the eye of all those that espy the *Daedong yeojido* is the dramatic mountain ridges used to describe Korea. Rather than expressing Korea's mountains as independent mountain peaks, Kim chose to describe them as connected mountain ridges as part of his efforts to capture the essence of the ki - energy that flows throughout the Korean peninsula. The lively mountain ridges are the result of advanced printmaking techniques. Meanwhile, the refined manner in which the roads and rivers are rendered, as well as the organized means through which the geographic signs are displayed demonstrate the degree of sophistication which had already been achieved during this period in terms of printmaking works. Kim Jeong-ho was thus not only a great geographer, but also a tremendous printmaker. Furthermore, he was a great artist who demonstrated the artistic values of atlases.

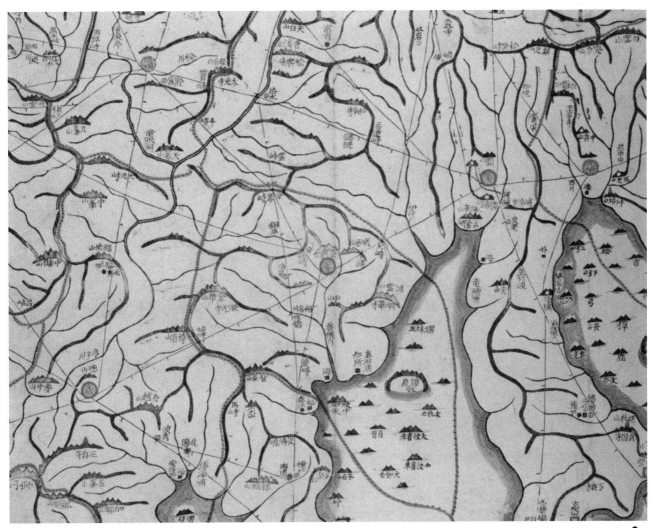

Hwangto: The Soil that Encompasses the Essence of Koreans

Hwangto (yellow soil) has long been an integral element in the daily lives and emotions of Koreans. Korean hwangto features more of a reddish hue than a yellow one. If one wanted to be more precise, he or she could claim that it is reddish soil in which a yellowish tint has been embedded. Its beautiful color and lyrical image have been emblazoned on the hearts and souls of Koreans.

Hwangto possesses a very poetic image. To this end, many Korean bards have written poems that have featured hwangtotgil (yellow soil road). The hwangtotgil found in these poems is one to which a great sense of sadness has been attached. This road has been used a metaphor for the weary life of the minjung (people). Thus, these poets expressed the sadness and difficulties of everyday life by comparing it to a hwangtotgil.

Although the image of hwangto is a very sad one, it is also one that is very familiar to Koreans. In the past, Koreans lived in houses made of hwangto, and ate foods that had been preserved in earthenware made out of the same material. Hwangto-made houses are believed to possess the inane ability to not only preserve warmth in winter and remain cool in summer, but also to automatically regulate humidity. In addition, the heating up of hwangto results in the emission of low intensity infrared rays which help ensure good blood circulation and the overall preservation of one's health by heating up the blood in the human body. However, the modern era has seen the disappearance of many of these hwangto-made structures.

Fortunately, the growing interest in health has resulted in once again drawing attention to the intrinsic values of hwangto. As a result, many goods fabricated out of hwangto, such as hwangto-beds, hwangto-cosmetics, and hwangto-dyed cloths have appeared on the market. Due to their alleged ability to restore vitality to tired and weary bodies, hwangto - jjimjilbang (a term which essentially denotes gender-segregated public bathhouse) have recently enjoyed a spike in popularity amongst Koreans. The number of people desiring to feel the mysterious power of the hwangto by building houses made out of this unique soil has also expanded significantly.

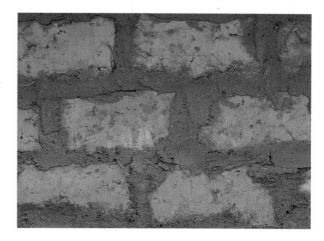

Gaetbeol: The Lungs of the Sea

Gaetbeol (mudflat) is a term which refers to the wide flat fields found in coastal areas. Located between the inland area and the sea, gaetbeol effectively connect the inland and maritime ecosystems. For a gaetbeol to be established, the slope of the coastline should be gentle and the gap between ebb and flow large. Furthermore, a significant amount of deposits must be pushed in from the sea. The South and West Coasts of Korea feature conditions which naturally lend themselves to the creation of such gaetbeol. The fame of Korean gaetbeol has spread the world over. Korean gaetbeol cover an area of some 2,393km², and account for almost 2.4% of Korea's overall territory.

The gaetbeol has long served as the basis of fishermen's lives. It has been a virtual maritime garden from which people have collected marine products such as clams and octopuses. The economic value of Korean gaetbeol has been estimated at over 10 billion dollars a year.

Gaetbeol are both the lungs of the sea and the treasure chest of the ecosystem. They represent one of the many natural resources which Korea can proudly boast about on the international stage. As gaetbeol are situated at the intersection where the sea's ebbs and flows push in and out, an abundance of oxygen and organic substances are created that provide sustenance for various kinds of organisms. In fact, the majority of fish and shellfish obtain their food from gaetbeol, and these ar-eas serve as their natural breeding grounds. Gaetbeol can thus rightfully be likened to the mother's womb for marine organisms.

However, Korea's gaetbeol have gradually decreased since the 1960s. In the past, people used to reclaim the areas in which gaetbeol were found to make farmland. However, from the 1960s onwards industrial complexes and urban areas began to be established on these re-claimed lands. This trend was in large part the result of the fact that gaetbeol were regarded as areas subject to development. Fortunately, this trend has recently decreased as people have become increasingly aware of the ecological importance of gaetbeol. In this regard, people now realize that the protection of gaetbeol is more beneficial to mankind than their development.

Sonamu: The Granddaddy of All Trees

Sonamu (Pine) represents the spirit of Koreans. Moreover, the sonamu is widely perceived by Koreans as the granddaddy of all trees. One even finds a reference to the pine in the second verse of the Korean national anthem: "Eternally Namsan's pine trees stand like an armor sure, through whatever tempest or danger, as our symbol of strength." Koreans regularly feel overwhelmed by emotion whenever they reach this passage. The sonamu is also perceived as a symbol of integrity and honor. As fall approaches, the leaves begin to fall from trees. However, the sonamu retains its emerald-colored integrity even in the depth of winter. Korean poets regularly wrote poems in which the notions of integrity and honor were compared to the sonamu.

Foreign nationals with a profound understanding of Korea have regularly referred to its residents as the people of the pine. This is because the sonamu has been deeply rooted in Koreans lives. In the olden days, Koreans were born in houses made out of sonamu; played around a garden in which sonamu had been planted; and used sonamu to heat their houses. They also made tteok or songpyeon (Korean rice cake) scented with pine leaves during the Chuseok (Korean Thanksgiving) holiday. In addition, they used furniture made of sonamu and appreciated paintings featuring its great beauty. When they passed away, people were buried in coffins made of sonamu. They even planted sonamu around their ancestors' graves.

Why have Koreans attempted to surround themselves by sonamu? While Koreans have always regarded sonamu as the granddaddy of all trees, they have also desired to inherit its lofty spirit and strong integrity. As such, Koreans have always attempted to live their lives surrounded by these majestic trees. Although the number of sonamu forests has decreased due to the influence of industrialization, the sonamu remains beloved by Koreans.

40 sonamu have been designated as Natural Monuments of Korea. Each of these was planted some 400 - 500 years ago. The kings of Joseon Dynasty (1392 - 1910) regularly granted government posts to sonamu. For instance, the sonamu that stands at the entrance to Beopjusa Temple in Songnisan Mountain is a famous tree that was granted senior grade of second court rank (jeong 2-pum) by King Sejo (the 7th king of the Joseon Dynasty) in 1464. Koreans have long communicated with nature through these sonamu, from whom they have also learned the wisdom and principles of worldly affairs.

Pungsu: A Philosophy Seeking to Achieve Coexistence with Nature

Pungsu (feng-shui or geomancy) is an environmental philosophy in which the wisdom that Koreans have accumulated over the years has become embedded. Koreans have never regarded land as a mere plot of soil and stones. In this regard, Koreans also believe that humans are an integral part of nature. As such, they have regarded the achievement of harmony between man and nature as being of great importance.

While pung means 'wind' su denotes 'water'. More specifically, wind refers to the climate and natural features, while water means the origin of life or survival. That being said, pungsu means much more that wind and water. Viewed from the broader perspective, pungsu refers to nature itself. Pungsu thus refers to a method through which humans seek to bring about an environment that is conducive to the living of a better existence. Koreans believe that nature is endowed with its own energy. More to the point, they believe that building a house on a site where the underground energy has congregated ensures prosperity for ensuing generations. They have also believed that the power of the state will be enhanced when the capital is established on such a site where the energy flows. Koreans also regard such places with mountains or hills in the back and rivers, streams or lakes in the front as a good place to live. This kind of topographical site is referred to in geomancy as baesan imsu-style land. The mountain or hill in the back stops the wind from blowing and protects the energy of the earth. Meanwhile, the water in front stops the energy of the earth originating from the mountain from being scattered. Water means fields on which grains can be grown. Therefore, the baesan imsu-style land is considered to be a comfortable and abundant place for people to live in. Seoul represents a perfect example of baesan imsu-style land. Seoul is a city which features the rugged features of Mt. Bukhansan to the north and the majestic Hangang River in front. Firmly within the embrace of Mt. Bukhansan, Seoul has also enjoyed vitality and abundance that has been granted to it by the Hangang River. In actuality, Seoul has enjoyed a special status as Korea's central city for over 2,000 years.

Pungsu is an integral part of the philosophy through which Koreans view nature. The belief that nature is not an object that can be conquered but rather the basis of humanity lies at the heart of pungsu. Pungsu is thus both a methodology for Koreans to use nature, and a philosophy to achieve harmony and coexistence with nature.

Doseongdo, apainting of Seoul during the Joseon Dynasty(1392-1910). As seen from the picture, Seoul is surrounded by mountains and water.

Cheonsang yeolcha bunyajido:
A Wondrous Depiction of the Skies

Koreans have long been enamored with gazing up at the sky. Ancient Koreans believed that climate changes could be predicted based on the flows of the sky. As the ability to predict the weather was very important to Koreans during the agricultural era, astronomy naturally has deep roots in Korea. To this end, the *Cheonsangyeolcha bunyajido* can be regarded as a piece which succinctly exhibits the high level of sophistication achieved by Korean astronomy. Cheonsang literally means "all the constellations in the sky."

Yi Seong-gye (King Taejo) was the individual who launched the coup that destroyed the Goryeo Dynasty (918 - 1392) and who subsequently founded the Joseon Dynasty (1392 - 1910). Attempting to find a symbol that could help to legitimize Joseon, Yi came across an astronomical map dating back to the Goguryeo Kingdom era (37 BC - 668). In this regard, Goguryeo Kingdom is known to have possessed a very advanced astronomical philosophy. For instance, constellations often appear on the ceilings of Goguryeo tomb murals. The astronomical maps contained in these Goguryeo murals demonstrate the high level of sophistication that had been achieved by Goguryeo Kingdom in terms of astronomy.

In 1395, Yi Seong-gye ordered the scholar Kwon Geun (1352 - 1409) to create a new astronomical map that was to be based on the Goguryeo one. Designed to inform the people that the foundation of Joseon Dynasty was in fact a mandate from heaven, this astronomical map eventually became known as the *Cheonsangyeolcha bunyajido*. One historical record concerned with the creation of this *Cheonsangyeolcha bunyajido* states that it was manufactured by complementing and partially modifying the constellations found in Goguryeo's astronomical map using a brass rubbing technique.

The *Cheonsangyeolcha bunyajido* is embedded with the independent spirit of Koreans. For instance, one can observe many constellations that are not found in China's *Shunyou tianwentu* (1247), which has widely been perceived as the oldest astronomical map in the world. In addition, the location of the constellations is also different from that found in the Chinese map. This is simply because the point of observation was Korea rather than China. The *Cheonsangyeolcha bunyajido* was manufactured from the standpoint of 39 degrees north latitude. This latitude runs near Goguryeo Dynasty 's capital on the Korean peninsula: Pyeongyang.

Describing 1,464 stars in 290 constellations, the *Cheonsangyeolcha bunyajido* is the second oldest astronomical map in the world. Gazing at this sophisticated scene of the skies, one can't help but be awestruck by the fact that the wisdom and scientific mindset of Koreans has been incorporated in this map.

Tiger: Spirit of Koreans

The children of Korea regard the tiger as a friendly animal. This is because the majority of the stories they hear from adults begin with the phrase "A long, long time ago when a tiger used to smoke····." Koreans of old regarded tigers as a godlike animal that drove away evil spirits and prevented disasters. Tigers were also worshiped in folk religions.

The Korean tiger is a kind of Siberian tiger indigenous to the Northeast Asian region. As the great majority of these tigers congregated in the area around Baekdusan Mountain, they also came to be known as Baekdusan tigers. Every Baekdusan Tiger's territory consisted of about 25km. The fact that the Baekdusan Mountain tiger had to adjust to precipitous mountainous areas as well as rapidly changing temperatures helped to instill in it a certain level of bravery and intelligence rarely found in other tigers. In this regard, records of conversations with hunters during the 19th century indicate that the Baekdusan Mountain tiger was more difficult to catch than other tigers in Asia. However, the spread of gun-based hunting in the 20th century had the effect of pushing the Baekdusan Mountain tiger to the brink of extinction.

Japan started to maliciously attack Baekdusan Mountain tigers during the Japanese colonial era(1910 - 1945). Designed to crush the spiritual world of Koreans, this Japanese offensive resulted in approximately 100 tigers being either shot to death or captured on the Korean peninsula during this period. The last wild tiger in South Korea was shot to death in a mountain in Gyeongju, Gyeongbuk Province in 1921. In 1993, three tigers were captured alive on the slopes of Nangnimsan Mountain on Jagang-Do Province of the North Korea. One of these three tigers was subsequently bequeathed to South Korea as a gift by the North. This tiger currently lives in Seoul Grand Park.

Tigers have often appeared as the main characters in Korean folklore and folk paintings. In folk stories of old, tigers were either treated as a courteous animal or degraded to the status of a silly animal that could easily be tricked. In addition, tigers are also described as entity that possesses the uncanny ability to transform itself into a man. Tigers have coexisted with Koreans since time immortal. In fact, a tiger character by the name of 'Hodori' was even selected as the mascot for the 1988 Olympic Games in Seoul. A friendly tiger, Hodori was meant to reflect the long tradition of friendliness and hospitality in Korea.

Hanwu: Friend of One's Lifetime

Hanwu is the term used to refer to indigenous Korean cows. Prior to the advent of industrialization, Koreans livelihoods were intricately related to that of cows. For them, cows were more than a mere form of livestock; they were in fact nothing less than a member of the family. The hanwu represented an important source of labor, provided a means of transportation, and took on many of the attributes of an emergency fund that could be tapped into when families fell on hard times. In olden days, a family that possessed many cows was regarded as a 'rich family'. The following poem about a cow is taken from the Korean textbook for third graders in elementary school.

A cow always eats slowly no matter how hungry it is
A cow always walks slowly even when it rains
A cow is slow to smile after a glorious event has emerged
A cow is slow to moan after a sad event has emerged
Cows may be slow, but it is this slowness that constitutes their genuine strength. Cows boast a warm and modest personality and are very patient animals. It is these very characteristics that make cows look slow. As can be seen from the poem, Koreans developed a strong understanding of cows' lives. The close proximity between man and cow in the past helped Koreans to forge a profound comprehension of the cow's happiness and sadness.

In olden days, Koreans regularly prepared meals consisting of beef, pork, or chicken whenever they had a party. Those parties that featured food made of beef were widely regarded as the best ones. Even after it has died, a cow continues to help its owner by leaving behind thick and tough leather that People can use to make clothes, bags, shoes, and even drums.

Bulgogi and Galbi can be regarded as representative Korean beef-based dishes. Bulgogi is a dish that consists of sliced beef that is both marinated and grilled. Meanwhile, Galbi guyi is a dish made of marinated and grilled 6 - 7cm long beef ribs, and Galbijjim is a dish created by marinating the beef ribs and then letting them boil in water for a long period of time. In addition, Galbitang is a soup made with beef ribs, radish, thick green onions, garlic, and ginger that is boiled for a long period of time. Beef ribs help restore the spleen and stomach's functions, stop vomiting and diarrhea, and reduce edema. These are also known to help strengthen muscle and bone texture.

Jindotgae: Korea's Indigenous Dog

Jindo is an island located in the southwest of the Korean peninsula. Jindo is renowned as an artistic island rich in traditional music, dance, and art. However, Jindo's main claim to fame is as the home of the indigenous Korean dog known as the 'Jindotgae dog'. The ancestry of the Jindotgae dog can be traced back to the Stone Age. Indigenous to Korea, the Jindotgae dog was able to maintain its bloodline and wild nature amidst the unique island environment. The Korean government officially registered the Jindotgae dog as a Korean cultural property and designated it as Korean Natural Monument No. 53 in 1962. The Jindotgae dog possesses a great character. It is especially loyal, obedient, brave and endowed with a great sense of smell; all qualities perceived as being very useful for hunting. In this regard, Koreans have regarded the Jindotgae dog as a naturally-gifted hunting dog.

The Jindotgae dog possesses a strong loyalty toward its owner. Once it has adopted a person as its owner, it will never betray him or her. These traits are linked to the breed's mysterious basic instinct to always attempt to return home. In fact, if one were to bring a Jindotgae dog some 300km away, over mountains and sea, it would always find a way to come back to its owner, whether it be by jumping aboard a passenger ship or swimming back to shore. One can only imagine how smart the Jindotgae dog is. In addition, the Jindotgae dog never eats food scraps without having permission from its owner. Although its loyalty toward its owner is strong, it remains very aggressive toward others. It never allows its guard to drop for even a moment. Furthermore, it is very clean and never relieves itself anywhere outside of its designated area.

The Jindotgae dog is characterized by its excellent sense of smell, endurance, and bravery. In other words, it possesses the basic qualities for hunting. The Jindotgae dog has reached such a degree of fame around the world that it has now been registered with England's Kennel Club (KC) and France's Federation Cynologique Internationale (FCI). In this regard, the state has gone to great lengths to preserve the Jindotgae dog's bloodline.

Cheukwugi: World's First Rain Gauge

Floods and drought are natural disasters which can difficultly be overcome based on human labor alone. With this in mind, Koreans began from early onwards to attempt to develop scientific methods to help them better cope with meteorological phenomena. In this regard, the most important task at that time was that of identifying the exact amount of rainfall. It was against this backdrop that the Cheukwugi (1441) was invented.

Cheukwugi is a gauge that measures the amount of rain which has fallen. The term Cheukwugi first appeared in the Sejong sillok, or annals of the reign of the Joseon dynasty's King Sejong (r. 1418 - 1450). These annals tell how rainfall was precisely measured using a jucheok (rainfall gauge) once the rain had stopped, and the dates on which the rain started and stopped were thereafter recorded.

The Cheukwugi used during this period consisted of an iron-made cylinder that stood 32cm tall and spanned 15cm in diameter. The length of the jucheok was about 21cm. It was during this period that the measurement of rainfall using a Cheukwugi began to be implemented nationwide, and that the measured rainfall was statistically estimated. Locally compiled statistics were regularly reported to the central government, and the total rainfall nationwide was then precisely recorded and preserved.

No other country besides Korea possessed the ability to scientifically measure rainfall during the 1400s. In fact, rainfall was only first scientifically measured in Italy in 1639, 1658 in France and 1677 in England. Invented well before Galileo's thermometer and Torricelli's barometer, the Cheukwugi thus represents the world's first rain gauge. The remains of a Cheukwugi manufactured during late Joseon Dynasty have been designated as National Treasure No. 561 and housed by the Korea Meteorological Administration.

Jagyeongnu and Angbuilgu:
Devices with which to Tell Time

Joseon Dynasty (1392 - 1910) was a country which was based on agriculture. Therefore, a great amount of attention was paid to astronomy, weather changes, time, and seasons. The fourth king of Joseon, King Sejong (reign 1418 - 1450), focused much of his energy on inventing various scientific devices through which nature could be observed, and on taking care of his people. King Sejong particularly desired to find ways to tell time in an exact fashion so as to help advance public life through the advent of scientific methods.

During the Joseon dynasty, the gates of fortresses were regularly closed whenever the bell announcing injeong (10:00 pm) rang, and opened when the bell announcing paru (4:00 am) tolled. Once the gates closed, patrollers went about checking the people walking around at night. However, there were many instances in which those responsible for ringing the bell failed to do so in a precise fashion. To rectify this situation, King Sejong ordered Jang Yeong-sil, who was the greatest scientist at that time, to manufacture a clock that could tell the exact time without having to depend on man. To this end, Jang Yeong-sil invented a highly-advanced water clock to measure time based on increases or decreases in the amount of water. This water clock featured an automatic time striking device, and was known as the Jagyeongnu.

The existing Jagyeongnu (National Treasure No. 229) was remanufactured in 1536.

The sundial was invented by Jang Yeong-sil, Yi Cheon, and Kim Jo. Originally called the Angbuilgu, the sundial was constructed in the shape of a hemisphere. In this regard, the center of the time board was hollow. It was designed to let the people know what time and season it was merely by looking at the end of the shadow created by the sunrise in the east and sunset in the west. The 13 parallel lines of latitude represent the 24 solar terms from the winter solstice to the summer solstice, and the 7 vertical lines represent the time. King Sejong ordered that these sundials be installed along busy streets so that the public could know what time it was during the day. Meanwhile, the water clock which featured an automatic time striking function was used to let people know the time at night.

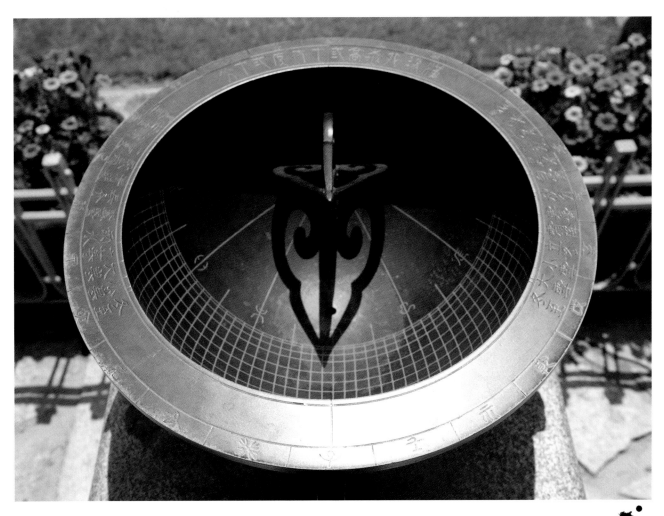

Geobukseon Ship: The World's First Armored Ship

As the world's first armored ship, the geobukseon (turtle ship) has always been a source of great pride for Koreans. The turtle ship combined the shipbuilding technology of the strong maritime power that was Silla Kingdom (57 BC - 935 AD) with the geomseon (an armored ship adorned with spears and swords located on the sides of the ship in order to prevent enemy ships from approaching) and gunfire technology of Goryeo Dynasty (918 - 1392), as well as the panokseon (an armored vessel which was covered in order to protect the soldiers during battle) technology of Joseon Dynasty (1392 - 1910).

The trutle ship was an armored attack vessel. Any discussion on the subject of the trutle ships must inherently include reference to one of the greatest individuals in Korean history: Admiral Yi Sun-sin (1545 - 1598). Yi focused on the production of such turtle ships as part of preparations for the Japanese invaders. Flanked by these turtle ships, he oversaw numerous victories against the Japanese naval forces during the Hideyoshi Invasions(1592 - 1598). In this regard, the Hansansando daecheop (Battle of Hansan) is widely regarded as one of the four most famous naval battles in world history. Many cadets from naval academies the world over have studied Yi Sun-sin's Hansando daecheop. Armed with loyalty, a lofty personality, and incredible leadership, Yi was able to save Joseon in its time of crisis. For his uncanny efforts and achievements, the Joseon government granted Yi the title of 'Chungmu'. The extent to which Yi has been idolized within Korean society is exemplified by the fact that his name and title have been used as the names of roads, subway stations, resorts, gyms, schools, and enterprises.

A turtle ship could accommodate approximately 130 people. 16 oars were installed on each side of the ship and 80 soldiers were in charge of pulling theses oars. Various methods of rowing were used to alter the direction of the ship based on the state of the battle. As such, the turtle ship boasted excellent mobility. A dragon-shaped head was adorned to the front of the turtle ship. In this regard, canons were fired through the mouth of this dragon head. In addition, spikes were installed on the turtle-shaped iron plates. This was designed to stop enemy soldiers from climbing aboard the ship and to prevent the emergence of hand-to-hand fighting.

The turtle ship featured a unique structure in that, while the outside world could be clearly seen from the inside, the inside was not visible from the outside. This structure provided an advantage to Korean forces while putting enemy forces at an obvious disadvantage. About 40 guns and artillery pieces were installed on the turtle ship and used to fire bombs and fire arrows toward the enemy forces. The turtle ship, which was armoured with iron plates and various bombs and fire arrows, could easily approach the center of enemy forces. Powerless before these turtle ships, the Japanese naval forced concentrated their energy on bidding a hasty retreat. The victories scored by the turtle ship during the Hideyoshi Invasions were much more than simple victories in battle, they constituted a victory for Koreans' creative spirit.

A miniature geobukseon (turtle ship).

Suwon Hwaseong Fortress:
Fulfilling King Jeongjo's Dream

Stretching 5.74km in length, Hwaseong Fortress is located in the Korean city of Suwon in Gyeonggi-Do Province. The fortress was constructed at the behest of the 22nd king of Joseon Dynasty (1392 - 1910), Jeongjo, following the latter's relocation of his father Prince Sado's grave to Suwon. Actual construction of the structure began in January 1794 and was completed in September 1796. The Suwon Hwaseong Fortress was the result of a combination of traditional Eastern and Western styles of architecture. Its architectural significance has resulted in it being evaluated as the epitome of fortress construction during the 18th century. In this regard, while the outer parapets are made of stone and brick, the inner parapets are filled with earth.

The Suwon Hwaseong Fortress was designed to function as a multipurpose city. More to the point, while it could accommodate public life, it could also be transformed into a place from which battles could be conducted whenever a national emergence occurred. This masterpiece created by King Jeongjo exudes an innate harmony in terms of its ability to balance the artificial and natural worlds, its functionality and artistic characteristics, and the combination of its usual and emergency functions.

King Jeongjo conducted politics in the most brutal and solitarily manner of all the kings of Joseon. Unwillingly dragged into political intrigue, his father (Prince Sado) met with a tragic death before he could even ascend the throne. Having himself been caught up in the conflicts between political factions, King Yeongjo, who was the grandfather of King Jeongjo, resorted to killing his own son by sealing him alive in a large rice chest. Ostensibly killed because of his involvement in an attempt to mount a palace coup, Prince Sado was in fact murdered at the behest of conservative forces who opposed his reformist agenda. As soon as he ascended the throne, King Jeongjo also found himself being challenged by these conservative factions, who called into question the legitimacy of the rule of a man who was in fact the son of a recognized criminal. King Jeongjo immediately began to dream about creating a new political space that lay outside of Seoul, where the existing power group resided. Simultaneously, he felt that this new space should be incorporated with his reformist ideas and compassion for the people. In this regard, Suwon Hwaseong Fortress can be regarded as the actualization of King Jeongjo's desires. In fact, his reforming spirit and compassion for the people constitute the very foundation of this large and beautiful fortress. As a result, King Jeongjo has, along with King Sejong, been regarded by Koreans as one of the most respected and beloved kings. The Suwon Hwaseong Fortress proudly boasts the cultural and scientific capabilities of Joseon during the late 18th century. To this end, many prestigious architects have picked the Suwon Hwaseong Fortress as the epitome of Asian fortresses. Its structure boasts the scientific and rational features needed to simultaneously satisfy functions related to military defense, everyday life, and commercial activities.

In accordance with the high praise for its scientific, architectural, artistic, military, and humanist elements, UNESCO included the Suwon Hwaseong Fortress on its World Cultural Heritage list in 1997. The *Hwaseong seongyeok uigwe*, a report which detailed the manner in which the structure was constructed, played a major role in having the Hwaseong Fortress registered on the World Cultural Heritage list. This report described the blueprint and progression of the construction of the fortress; however, it also included the construction technology employed, construction methods utilized, machines and equipment used, the means through which raw materials were processed, construction logs, budgets and wages, as well as personal information about the laborers. Pictures were also added to provide additional explanations. Such detailed, complete, and multi-dimensional construction reports cannot be found in places such as St. Petersburg and Washington, which also feature buildings constructed during the same period as the Suwon Hwaseong Fortress. This report can thus rightfully be regarded as another Suwon Hwaseong Fortress constructed on paper.

IT: Change the Korean's Lifestyle

The use of the term IT first began to be popular during the middle of the 1990s in Korea. A mere 10 years has since elapsed, during which time Korea has already become the world's leading IT powerhouse. A full 1/3 of the mobile phones, digital TVs, and semiconductors currently found in the global market were produced by Korean enterprises. Korea also ranks 1st or 2nd in the world in terms of Internet penetration and the use of personal computers and mobile phones. Moreover, from 2007 onwards, Korean communications enterprises even began to provide their clients with moving picture services over their mobile phones. In other words, we have now entered an era in which people can actually see the person they are talking to on their mobile phones. Within the first year, some 10 million people had already subscribed to this moving picture service. Korea was also the first to introduce a wireless internet service that makes possible the use of high-speed internet even when while travelling by automobile or train.

Korea's emergence as a global IT powerhouse has been the result of aggressive efforts on the part of the government. The Kim Dae-jung and Roh Moo-hyun administrations in particular invested heavily in the establishment of the infrastructure needed for Korea to develop its IT industry. High-speed communication networks were established nationwide. The government also provided subsidies that made it possible for the public to purchase computers at low prices. It has also provided widespread support to IT and venture companies. This comprehensive effort has led to the development of world-class information and communications, computer, semiconductor, software, game, and contents industries. These endless efforts on the part of the government and enterprises, as well as consumers' thirst for IT related goods, have resulted in Korea becoming the leading IT power in the world.

IT is no longer just an industry in Korea; it has become a way of life and developed a culture of its own. The advent of IT has also altered Korea's political, social, and cultural structure. This IT's incorporation of such elements as the media, publishing, and moving pictures, to say nothing of education and shopping, has effectively ushered in a brave new world for Koreans.

History, Cites, People

Dolmen / Comb-pattern pottery / Seoul / Gyeongju / Pyeongyang / The DMZ /
Seokguram Grotto / Street Cheering / Dangun / King Gwanggaeto / Wonhyo / King Sejong /
Admiral Yi Sun-sin / Jeong Yak-yong / Yi Hwang / An Jung-geun / Yu Gwan-sun

Dolmen: Stones of Spirit

Dolmens are the remains of a megalithic culture established about 3,000 years ago. The dolmen, essentially graves made of stone, were common throughout Europe and Asia. About 30,000 dolmens can be found on the Korean peninsula. Dolmen represents a historical code through which the Bronze Age can be explained.

A cultural legacy of the Bronze Age, Korean dolmens can rightfully be compared to the Pyramids, Obelisk, and Stone Hedge. These can be regarded as vital sources of information on the spiritual world, social structure, and political system of those who lived during that age and worshiped huge stones, as well as on the culture and lifestyle that prevailed during the prehistoric era.

The elite during the Bronze Age possessed so much influence that they were able to have large numbers of people mobilized to build their graves. The higher the status of the person, the more impressive the size and scale of the stone was. While smaller ones weighed about 10 tons, the larger ones weighed in excess of 300 tons. A look at these house-sized dolmens leaves the beholder to contemplate the authority of those for whom such monuments were built.

Dolmens can broadly be classified into the Northern and Southern styles. Because of its table-like shape, the northern-style of dolmen is also referred to as the table style. Meanwhile, the southern style dolmen is often called the checkerboard style. Remains were found from Korean dolmens. These include stone swords, stone arrowheads, mandolin-shaped daggers, bronze axes, bronze arrowheads, and adornments. These mandolin-shaped daggers believed to have been used by the elite are regarded as being representative of the Bronze Age. There are currently about 30,000 dolmens in Korea. In this vein, various styles of dolmens that cannot be found anywhere else can be found in the Gochang, Hwasun, and Ganghwa areas. Regarded as exhibiting the technology and social phenomenon of the prehistoric era, the dolmens in these areas have been registered by UNESCO as World Cultural Heritages. These prehistoric dolmens have helped Korea acquire a reputation around the globe as the country of dolmens.

Comb-pattern pottery: The Root of Korean Ceramics

Comb-pattern pottery is usually associated with the Neolithic Age. In this particular art form, comb patterns are inlaid on the surface of the pottery pieces. In general, comb-pattern pottery boasts one of two shapes: a narrow-bottomed oval or broad bottomed shape. These pieces were made by heating the clay in a kiln at a temperature of 600°c - 700°c. Some of the pieces which have been recovered to date include pots, jars, bowls, and small bowls. In this regard, while large pieces were mostly used for storage purposes, the medium ones were used for cooking, and the small ones as utensils.

Koreans have attached many meanings to this comb-pattern pottery. For instance, it has simultaneously been perceived as remains symbolic of the Neolithic Age and as the root of Korean ceramics. Viewed from this standpoint, it can rightfully be regarded as the mother of Korean blue and white celadon.

Korea is not the only place where such comb-pattern pottery has been discovered. This type of pottery in fact has been found on the Korean peninsula, in Manchuria, the Mongol Steppe, and even as far away as Lake Baikal in Russia. In addition, pieces have also been discovered along the Volga River that lies over the Ural Mountains as well as in the Northern European nation of Finland. No one knows from where this comb-pattern pottery originated, or the manner in which it spread. What is clear however is that comb-pattern pottery represents a clear sign of significant cultural exchanges between East and West. Koreans are very proud of the fact that their ancestors were a part of this early attempt at cultural exchanges through comb-pattern pottery, and that ensuing generations were able to develop high-tech ceramics based on these ancient art forms.

Seoul: The Soul of Asia

Seoul is the capital city of Korea. It is an ancient city with a 2,000-year history that has become one of the major hubs in Northeast Asia. People first began to live in the Seoul area during the Neolithic Age. This fact is substantiated by the pottery pieces and remnants of residential areas that have been uncovered in the Amsa-dong, Gangdong-gu area of Seoul. Seoul first began to appear in historical records during the Baekje Kingdom era (18 BC - 660 AD). The founder of the Baekje Kingdom, Onjo, selected the area south of the Hangang River as his capital. In this regard, the remains of Pungnap toseong and Mongchon toseong were found in modern-day Songpa-gu, Seoul. Historians have estimated that these two sites were home to the palaces of Baekje. One can find royal tombs from early Baekje Kingdom near these earthen walls.

Seoul effectively became a part of the hotly disputed border between Goguryeo Kingdom (37 BC - 668 AD), Baekje Kingdom, and Silla Kingdom (57 BC - 935 AD) when Baekje Kingdom moved its capital to modern-day Gongju in Chungnam Province in 475. The three kingdoms were subsequently involved in a ferocious competition for control of the Seoul area that lasted until the end of the 600s. General Yi Seong-gye destroyed the Goryeo dynasty (918 - 1392) and founded a new dynasty called Joseon (1392 - 1910). To this end, Seoul regained its former glory after the rulers of Joseon Dynasty selected it, which they referred to as Hanyang, as their capital.

Seoul was able to overcome the ravages of the Japanese colonial era (1910 - 1945) and the subsequent Korean War (1950 - 53) and rapidly become the center of the Korean economic and cultural revival. It has now grown into an international city, as exemplified by its successful hosting of the 1988 Seoul Olympics and the 2002 Korea-Japan World Cup.

The Hangang River separates Seoul into northern and southern areas. The northern bank of the Hangang River is regarded as the old downtown area. It is home to the official residence of the President (Cheongwadae), government offices, embassies, several Joseon-era palaces (Gyeongbokgung Palace, Changdeokgung Palace, Changgyeonggung Palace, Deoksugung Palace, and Gyeongheegung Palace), the National Museum of Korea, National Folk Museum of Korea, City Hall, Namdaemun Market, Dongdaemun Market, Myeongdong, Insadong, and Itaewon.

The southern bank of the Hangang River has emerged as a new downtown area, the great majority of which was developed since the 1970s. The area is home to large apartment complexes, businesses, and several fashion industry-related stores. Moreover, the Seoul Trade Exhibition Center, Korea City Air Terminal, as well as several large domestic and foreign enterprises, hotels and department stores also call this area home. A

21st century-type underground city called the COEX Mall has been constructed under the Seoul Trade Exhibition Center. This underground city consists of a multiplex cinema, large bookstore, an aquarium, restaurants, fashion stores, cafes, and bars.

A metropolitan city home to more than 10 million people, Seoul has become one of the central cities of Northeast Asia. Seoul, a city rich in history and culture, is also the soul of Asia in the 21st century and a place where past and present coexist.

Gyeongju: The Rome of Korea

Gyeongju is widely regarded as the leading cultural city in Korea. It is to Koreans what Athens is to Greeks and Rome to Italians. Gyeongju was the capital of the Silla Kingdom (57 BC - 935 AD) for almost 1,000 years. The extent of the cultural properties, remains, and relics from the Silla Kingdom found in the city has led people to refer to it as a historical time capsule.

Gyeongju experienced an even greater era of development during the period that followed Silla's unification of the Three Kingdoms. Silla's victory over Baekje Kingdom (18 BC - 660 AD) and Goguryeo Kingdom (37 BC - 668 AD) ushered in a period in which the conquerors successfully assimilated the culture, scientific technology, and political institutions of the other two kingdoms, each of which had been more advanced than Silla. It was during this unified period that the cultural legacies for which Gyeongju is most renowned were produced.

The majority of the center of Gyeongju has been designated as a national park. Over 7 million people visit Gyeongju every year to experience its cultural legacies. One can find in excess of 100 pieces which have been designated as national treasures and properties in Gyeongju. Above all, Gyeongju is home to Bulguksa Temple and Seokguram Grotto, two structures that have been regarded as the epitome of Buddhist culture, and to the Gyeongju Historic Areas registered on the World Cultural Heritage list.

Built in 774, Bulguksa Temple is located in the middle of Tohamsan Mountain in the southeast of Gyeongju. It is a unique temple whose buildings embody the paradise and ideal world described in the Buddhist Scriptures. Similar Buddhist structures are difficult to come across anywhere else in Asia. It is quite simply a temple of breathtaking formative and artistic beauty.

Seokguram Grotto, a dome-style cave made of natural rock in which a statue of Buddha has been preserved, is widely regarded as the acme of Buddhist art during the heyday of the Silla Kingdom. Created during the same period as Bulguksa Temple, it is a Buddhist sculpture of monumental magnitude that combines the essence of architecture, irrigation, geometry, religious passion, and artistic spirit. The Gyeongju Historic Areas provide a panorama of the 1,000 year history and culture of the Silla Kingdom. Pagodas and Buddhist statues, palace sites, royal tombs, Buddhist temple sites, and fortresses can all be espied within these areas. The density and diversity of the cultural remains found in the Gyeongju Historic Areas has led some to claim that the city has more to offer in this regard than the traditional Japanese cities of Kyoto and Nara.

Pyeongyang: The Capital of North Korea

Located in the northwest of the Korean peninsula, Pyeongyang is one of the oldest cities in Korea. It was the last capital of the first Korean kingdom: Gojoseon (2333 BC - 108 BC). Gojoseon was an ancient state whose territory spanned from the northeastern reaches of China to the northern part of the Korean peninsula. During the 4th century BC Gojoseon relocated its capital to Pyeongyang, or Asadal as it was known at the time.

The collapse of Gojoseon was followed soon thereafter by the rise of a new kingdom named Goguryeo Kingdom (37 BC - 668 AD) which occupied the northeast reaches of China and northern part of the Korean peninsula. While Pyeongyang was one of the most vibrant cities in the southern reaches of Goguryeo Kingdom, the Kingdom initially established its capital in the modern-day Chinese city of Jian. In 427, or some 500 years after the establishment of the dynasty, Pyeongyang officially became the capital of Goguryeo. However, Pyeongyang was stripped of its status as the capital after Goguryeo Kingdom was defeated by the allied forces of the Tang dynasty (618 AD - 907 AD) of China and Silla Kingdom (58 BC - 935 AD) in 668. However, the city remained an important one during the Goryeo Dynasty (918 AD - 1392 AD) and Joseon Dynasty eras (1392 AD - 1910 AD). It eventually became the capital of North Korea following the official division of the nation in 1948. Pyeongyang is the third biggest city on the Korean peninsula after Seoul and Busan. It currently has a population of about 3.1 million people.

Like most historical cities, Pyeongyang is home to many remains and relics. It is home amongst others to cave relics from the Paleolithic Age, dolmens from the Bronze Age, and several Goguryeo tombs featuring beautiful mural paintings. The historical value of these mural paintings lies in the fact that they vividly depict the lifestyle and spiritual world of the ancient era. In this regard, UNESCO has included these Goguryeo tombs on the World Cultural Heritage list.

Pyeongyang was off limits to South Koreans for some 60 years following the division of the nation into South and North Korea. Fortunately, the successful holding of the 1st inter-Korean Summit in June 2000 has paved the way for South Koreans, albeit only a few, to visit Pyeongyang. South Koreans have long dreamt of the day when the country can be reunified and they can be free to finally set their eyes on the ancient city of Pyeongyang.

©imageclick

The DMZ: The Path to Reunification

Having officially divided the Korean peninsula into South and North Korea ever since the Korean War ended in July 1953, the DMZ (Demilitarized Zone) is an area that evokes great sadness amongst the Korean people. The DMZ truncates the Korean peninsula at its center (38th parallel), effectively dividing the nation into Southern and Northern parts. The DMZ spans 250km from east to west and 4km from north to south. Fortunately, the two sides have managed to avoid any huge conflagrations or even all-out war over the past 50 years.

The new century has ushered in some significant changes where the DMZ is concerned. The first ever inter-Korean summit held since the division served as the impetus for the opening, albeit partial, of the previously hermetically sealed DMZ on June 15th, 2000. Since then, roads cutting across the western and eastern reaches of the DMZ, which had been closed for the past 50 years, have been reopened to select traffic from South and North Korea.

South Korea has also established an industrial complex in the North Korean border city of Gaeseong. There are currently some 70 South Korean enterprises operating out of the Gaeseong Industrial Complex established over an area of 3.3km². Approximately 20,000 North Korean residents work in these factories. People, trucks, and trains have been plying the South and North Korean sides of the border while transporting the products made in Gaeseong.

The scale of the Gaeseong Industrial Complex is expected to increase to 66 km² in the future.

The Mt. Geumgangsan Tourist Area in North Korea has now become a primary destination for South Korean tourists. In fact, in excess of 100,000 South Korean people have in recent years travelled to Mt. Kumgangsan through the DMZ. In addition, the two leaders (South Korean President Roh Moo-hyun and the Chairman of the National Defense Commission Kim Jeong-il) also agreed during their summit held in October 2007 to expand the tourist program so as to also include the Gaeseong and Mt. Baekdusan area. Having long served as a symbol of division and war, the DMZ has now become the path to exchanges, reconciliation and reunification.

The DMZ area has remained off limits to all human traffic for more than 50 years. This has resulted in Koreans' inheriting a setting that has over time become a natural preserve the likes of which has rarely been seen anywhere else in the world. The DMZ is both an ecological treasure trove and a haven for wildlife.

Seokguram Grotto: The Essence of Buddhist Art

The Seokguram Grotto (Built in 774) is very hard to define with any exactitude. Much like it is impossible to adequately describe the moment a flower blooms or the sublimity of pure love, it is impossible to summarize the essence of the Seokguram Grotto in a few words. The Seokguram Grotto is both a masterpiece of Buddhist art and the epitome of religious passion, science, and fine art. It is also the only artificial grotto in the world. Seokguram itself consists of a rectangular antechamber and a main rotunda. Surprisingly, the main rotunda boasts a domed ceiling which symbolizes heaven; thus proving that the people of Silla Kingdom had already developed the notions of mathematics, symmetry, and mechanics needed to create a dome by piling up stones as early as 1,300 years ago.

The building of the Seokguram Grotto required the people of Silla to cut and customize an enormous number of stones. Each stone employed was both bulky and weighty, thus meaning that several people would have to work together to transport them. However, Silla craftsmanship did not allow for a margin of error of even 1mm when cutting the stones and placing them in the desired spot. According to research conducted by Korean scientists who measured the grotto at 10m intervals, the actual margin of error was less than 1/10,000. The overall degree of perfection of the Seokguram Grotto is as such in many ways the result of the faultlessness of its parts.

The people of Silla believed that while heaven was round, the earth was square. This astronomical outlook has been incorporated into the Seokguram Grotto, which consists of a rectangular antechamber and a main rotunda. Here, the rectangular antechamber can be perceived as representing the earth, while the main rotunda symbolizes heaven. Buddhist images represent the high point of Buddhist art. The Seokguram Grotto houses 38 images of divinities, including the seated main Buddha. While there were originally 40 Buddhist images in the Seokguram Grotto, two of these were stolen by Japanese colonial officials during the colonial era (1910 - 1945).

The Sakyamuni housed in the main rotunda, on which the image of a wise and benevolent Buddha is perfectly rendered, constitutes the main character in the Seokguram Grotto. Seokguram Grotto represents the essence of Silla Art. In addition, looking beyond its simple aesthetics, the grotto can be said to constitute a primary example of the outstanding nature of the architectural culture which existed in ancient Korea. Seokguram Grotto is thus a masterpiece from both an architectural and religious standpoint.

Evaluated as a fine masterpiece of Korean Buddhist art and as the only man-made grotto in the world, UNESCO made the decision to include the Seokguram Grotto on the World Cultural Heritage List in 1995.

Street Cheering: The Festival of Dynamism

The broad and long street (Sejongno) that runs from the square in front of Seoul City Hall to Gyeongbokgung Palace is known as the Agora of Korea. It was in this place that people gathered to call for freedom and democracy, calls that eventually resulted in the achievement of the democratization of Korea. The April 19 Revolution of 1961 and the June 10 Democratization Movement of 1987 were civic movements that changed the paradigm of Korean society. Although these two movements were carried out nationwide, symbolic performances were carried out in front of City Hall and Sejongno.

This place has been regarded as the Agora of Korea because of its historical aura. For over six hundred years this street has served as the country's political nerve center, and as the area in which all important government institutions have been located. This street was destined to become the nation's political center from 1394 onwards after Joseon Dynasty selected Seoul as its capital and began building palaces within the city.

In the summer of 2002, the Korea-Japan World Cup was held in several of Korea's major cities. All at once, the Agora of Korea was transformed into the street of festivals. The Korean soccer team finished 4th during the 2002 Korea-Japan World Cup. This unexpected result was in large part due to the passionate cheering of Koreans. Seoul citizens poured into the Agora square whenever the Korean soccer team was in action. This street cheering reached its peak during the semifinal match between Korea and Germany. The vivid images of hundreds of thousands of Korean citizens decked out in the red shirts emblematic of the Korean national side massing together to voice their support for the home team left an indelible impression in the hearts and minds of people the world over.

In the spring and summer of 2008, this street of festivals was once again transformed into an Agora where up to 100,000 people gathered at one time. The decision on the part of the conservative government inaugurated in 2008 to forego Korea's quarantine inspection sovereignty and the people's right to live a healthy life by concluding a lop-sided beef treaty with the United States resulted in the people filling the Agora with their candles of justice and democracy. Above all, the Korean public required that the government revoke these unilateral policies that failed to take into account public opinion.

As such, Sejongno has simultaneously served as an Agora and a festival street.

Image of the Sejongno and the square in front of Seoul City Hall flooded
with 'Red Devils' during the 2002 Korea-Japan World Cup

© Kwon Tae-kyun

Dangun: The Father of the Korean Nation

Gojoseon (2333 BC - 108 BC) was the first Korean kingdom ever formed. Located in the northeast of China and northern area of the Korean peninsula, Gojoseon was founded by Dangun, a historical figure that has taken on a very profound symbolic meaning to all Koreans. Dangun began to be revered as a figure of great symbolic significance during the Unified Silla period. At that time, Dangun played the role of binding the people of the three kingdoms together into one nation. The advent of the Goryeo Dynasty (918 - 1392) saw Dangun emerge as the father of the Korean nation in the consciousness of Koreans. During the 13th century, Goryeo Dynasty found itself faced with a national crisis in the form of an invasion from China's Yuan dynasty (1231 - 1270). During this period, Dangun served as an entity that provided hope to the people of Goryeo in their time of need. Later on, King Sejong (r. 1418 - 1450) of the Joseon Dynasty built the Dangun Shrine in Pyeongyang, and began to implement an ancestral ritual in his name.

The division of the two Koreas into South and North Korea has now endured for in excess of 60 years. Nevertheless, the two Koreas are able to trace their common heritage back to Dangun; moreover, the mutual respect and reverence displayed toward Dangun has spurred the two sides to try to move beyond their respective ideologies. South Korea has even designated and celebrated the date (October 3) on which Gojoseon was founded by Dangun as its National Day. Dangun's tomb is believed to be located in Pyeongyang.

Records related to the Dangun Myth can be found in the *Samguk yusa* (Legends and History of the Three Kingdoms of Ancient Korea) compiled by the monk Ilyeon in 1281. According to the myth, Hwanwung, who was the son of Hwanin (Heavenly King), descended from the heavens to live in the human world along with the wind, rain, clouds and three thousand of his loyal subjects. Hwanwung transformed a bear who desired to become human into a woman and married her. She later bore him a son named Dangun.

Koreans are very proud of Dangun and the Dangun Myth. To this end, Dangun is perceived as both the root and spiritual symbol of Koreans.

King Gwanggaeto: The Alexander of Asia

The 19th King of Goguryeo Kingdom (37 BC - 668 AD), King Gwanggaeto(r. 391 - 413) is regarded as a conquering king who ruled over the largest swathe of land ever associated with a Korean kingdom. Some have even labeled this potentate who held sway over the entire northeastern area of China and half of the Korean peninsula as the Alexander of Asia.

Ascending to the throne in 391, Gwanggaeto became the first king in Korean history to independently select his era name (yeonho). This yeonho, which was used to refer to the years in which a king reigned, was generally regarded as a means for kings to exhibit their political orientation. By independently selecting his era name, Gwanggaeto effectively served notice to his foreign and domestic audiences that Goguryeo Kingdom regarded itself as the equivalent of China.

Gwanggaeto was far and away one of the most dynamic leaders in Korean history. He successfully attacked the kingdom of Baekje (18 BC - 643 AD) located in the southern reaches of the Korean peninsula and assumed control over the central and westerns areas of the Korean peninsula. In addition, he also received tributes from Silla Kingdom, with whom he maintained a vassal-based relationship. He later conquered East Buyeo to the north and defeated the Later Yan (384 - 409, one of the sixteen kingdoms of five ethnic groups in China) to take effective control of the vast realm of Manchuria.

A Gwanggaeto Stele made of granite was uncovered in the city of Jian located in the northeast of China. His son King Jangsu had this monument constructed as a memorial to his deceased father. It stands 6.39m tall and 1.5m in width. The inscription on the stele lays out the multiple achievements of King Gwanggaeto in 1,775 characters. According to the inscription, King Gwanggaeto conquered 64 fortresses and 1,400 villages which were subsequently incorporated into the territory of Goguryeo Kingdom. Koreans are very proud of King Gwanggaeto whose orders were delivered as he rode his horse through the fields of Manchuria. He is rightfully idolized as a leader who ruled over the largest Korean kingdom.

Wonhyo: A Monk who Dreamt about Harmony

Wonhyo(617 - 686) was a Silla Kingdom era (57 BC - 935 AD) monk who has been credited with having greatly contributed to the opening of a new era of Korean Buddhism as well as to the spread of its tenets. In particular, he left behind a famous episode relating to a journey which he embarked on to study in the land of Tang. On his way to a port to board a ship in 661, he suddenly found himself being overcome by darkness. As there were no villages along his way, he was forced to spend the night in the mountains. Having found a cave to sleep in for the night, he found himself getting thirsty during his sleep.

Rummaging around, he located what he believed to be a gourd or bowl filled with water. After having partaken of its sweet nectar, he went back to sleep. When he woke up the next morning he found himself in a shallow grave and discovered that the object which he had thought was a gourd or bowl was actually a skull. Having in fact drunk dirty water from a skeleton, Wonhyo soon found himself falling sick and vomiting. While vomiting, he suddenly realized that every affair was in fact dependent on one's mind. As such, he realized that truth could be found from within oneself rather than externally. Convinced that it was no longer necessary for him to travel abroad to study because he had been enlightened, he returned home.

While the great majority of monks lived lives of luxury that involved tem never leaving the sanctity of their temples, Wonhyo spent his time amongst the public trying to promote the tenets of Buddhism. As part of his efforts to enlighten the people, he was prone to dance around while tapping a gourd and turning phrases from the Buddhist scriptures into songs. He also drank alcohol with the people, and regularly penned summaries of the Buddhist scriptures which he presented during public lectures.

Wonhyo strove to harmonize all worldly conflicts and contradictions. His philosophy of Buddhism, which was focused on the achievement of harmony, was not only conveyed to China but also played a pivotal role in the development of Hua-Yen Buddhism. Thus, the spirit of harmony sought by the Buddha Sakyamuni was recreated by Wonhyo some 1,200 years after his passing. For Koreans, Wonhyo represents much more than a great monk; for them, he was also an outstanding thinker and philosopher.

King Sejong: The Leonardo da Vinci of Korea

King Sejong (1397 - 1450) is widely regarded as the greatest king in Korean history, and also as one of the most outstanding individuals in the annals of world history. The fourth king of the Joseon dynasty (1392 - 1910), he is credited with having created the Korean writing system.

One of King Sejong's most remarkable achievements is the creation of 'Hangeul'. Hangeul is the only writing system in the world for which clear records detailing the period in which it was invented, the person who invented it, and the origins of the basic principles of the system, can be found. Linguists the world over have marveled at Hangeul, regarding it as one of the most unique, scientific, and rational language systems ever uncovered. The completeness of Hangeul was once again confirmed when UNESCO included it on its World Documentary Heritage list. The organization has also established the King Sejong Literacy Prize, which is awarded to those contributing to the eradication of illiteracy from the world. The reign of King Sejong marked the heyday of Joseon culture and philosophy. In 1420, King Sejong established an academic research institute within the palace called the Jiphyeonjeon. The reign of King Sejong was thus a period in which the foundation of modern Korean culture was established. King Sejong regarded the appointment of competent hu-

man resources as being of great importance. He was wont to employ individuals with outstanding talent and competencies, and this even if the latter did not belong to the aristocracy. In this regard, Jang Yeong-sil can be perceived as the consummate example of King Sejong's preference for the appointment of competent people. Jang Yeong-sil, who was from the lowborn class, has been lauded as the most brilliant scientist of the Joseon Dynasty era. There is even a Jang Yeong-sil Science High School in the international port city of Busan.

King Sejong has been identified by Koreans as one of the greatest people of all time. In this regard, he achieved many impressive things not only in the academic field, but also in various other sectors such as politics, economics, diplomacy, warfare, music, and publishing. The famous American author Pearl S. Buck, who took care of orphans and multiracial children in Korea from 1964 to 1973, once praised King Sejong as the "Leonardo da Vinci of Korea." Koreans have named numerous roads and research institutes, universities, and even publishing companies after Sejong. In addition, the portrait of King Sejong adorns Korea's 10,000 won bill. Koreans have thus celebrated the great King Sejong by attaching his name to a variety of items.

Admiral Yi Sun-sin: The Hero of All Koreans

Korea has navigated through numerous crises during its 5,000-year history. Of these crises, perhaps none were as serious as the Hideyoshi Invasions (1592 - 1598) that threatened to wrest Joseon Dynasty of its sovereignty. However, this crisis also set the stage for the emergence of a hero who risked it all to save his country and people. This man was none other than Admiral Yi Sun-sin (1545 - 1598) of Joseon Dynasty (1392 - 1910). Widely regarded as the greatest admiral in Korean history, Yi boasted an unbounded sense of loyalty, a lofty personality, and unrivalled leadership. Having incisively forecasted the Japanese invasion, Yi focused his energies on the training of his forces and the manufacturing of the legendary turtle ships. These turtle ships would later go on to play an important role in protecting the homeland during the Hideyoshi Invasions.

Admiral Yi Sun-sin engaged Japanese naval forces on 23 different occasions and emerged victorious every single time. In this regard, the Hansansando daecheop (Battle of Hansan) has been widely regarded as one of the four most famous naval battles in the world. Meanwhile, the Noryang haejeon (Battle of Noryang) is remembered by Koreans as one of the most bittersweet battles in the history of the nation. Although a significant victory was scored on that day, Yi was fatally wounded by an enemy bullet during the closing moments of the battle. During the final moments of his life Yi instructed his men, "Do not let the enemy know about my death." Thus even as he lay dying, he continued to exhibit a strong desire to do his best to save his country and people.

Yi was also a prolific writer. His most famous work, the *Nanjung ilgi* (War Diary of Admiral Yi Sun-sin), was a diary that vividly described life during the seven-year period marked by the Hideyoshi Invasions. Including a host of topics described in a sophisticated manner, the book deals with such themes as Admiral Yi's inner most thoughts on humanity, his love for his men and the people, his frank and honest advice with regards to national governance, and his dramatic descriptions of actual battles. He also left behind many beautiful poems.

Admiral Yi's portrait has been enshrined in Hyeonchungsa located in the city of Asan in Chungnam Province. Moreover, memorial services are regularly held for him there. Koreans continue to regard him as the greatest hero in the long history of the nation. His life has also served as a good source of inspiration for various art forms, including novels, movies, plays, musicals, and dramas.

Jeong Yak-yong: Korea's Premiere Intellectual

Korea proudly boasts two people who can rightfully be compared to Leonardo da Vinci: One is King Sejong, and the other is a reformer who lived during the Joseon Dynasty (1392 - 1910) by the name of Jeong Yak-yong. Jeong (1762 - 1836) has been hailed as the premiere intellectual of the day, and as a renaissance man who dabbled in philosophy, literature, ideology, science, architecture, politics, medical science, military matters, economics, history, and geography. Jeong was also an eminent Silhak scholar who attempted to introduce methods to improve the people's everyday lives. Silhak (Practical Learning) is a practical school of thought that was highly critical of what it perceived as the overly theoretical and doctrinal attributes of Neo-Confucianism. Silhak scholars promoted the use of scientific methods as a means of bringing about a society in which the people could actually draw enjoyment from their lives.

Any discussion of the life of Jeong Yak-yong must inevitably include mention of King Jeongjo (r. 1776 - 1800). As one of the leading lights of the Renaissance of Joseon Dynasty, King Jeongjo desired to overcome the social contradictions that had lingered since the middle ages. In this regard, while King Jeongjo dreamt of a new world, it was Jeong Yak-yong who undertook the task of actualizing it. Built as a result of the mobilization of all the capabilities at Jeong Yak-yong's disposal, the Hwaseong Fortress in Suwon was a multipurpose city that effectively gave form to King Jeongjo's long-held dream. Perfectly harmonizing the artificial and natural, functional and artistic, and combining emergency and everyday functions, the Suwon Hwaseong is regarded as King Jeongjo's masterpiece.

Jeong Yak-yong's thought was rooted in the notions of practicality and fairness. For instance, he adamantly believed that the members of the seonbi (literati class) should also engage in agriculture, industry, and commerce. More to the point, he advocated the fact that everyone, regardless of their social class, should participate in the production process, and that the products should be distributed in a fair way. We can see the utilitarianism and egalitarianism from his thoughts. Highly critical of Joseon society, which he viewed as looking down on those classes of people who possessed skills and techniques while putting those engaged in purely academic pursuits on a pedestal, Jeong firmly clung to the need for Joseon to introduce modern technologies from the Western world. Jeong's thinking was in many ways before its time, and as such ran contrary to many of the accepted tenets of the day. For instance, he clearly believed that the people had the right to replace a ruler whose actions ran contrary to the public good.

Jeong was keenly aware of the hardships faced by the people and did his utmost to make their dreams come true. However, the suspicious death of King Jeongjo resulted in throwing Jeong's life into crisis. This incident and the ensuing crackdown on Catholicism launched by the conservative faction that had long been critical of his thought resulted in Jeong Yak-yong being labeled a Catholic and exiled to Gangjin in Jeollanam-Do Province. Despite the obvious difficulties caused by his exile, Jeong used the opportunity to establish the Dasan chodang as part of his efforts to pass his knowledge on to his disciples. He also used this time to undertake a compilation of his studies. As such, he used this painful period of exile to pour his energy into educational, research, and compilation activities. During his 18-year exile, Jeong compiled over 50 books concerned with a variety of topics that ranged from politics, economics, law and medical science, to geography, history and literature. Jeong was a philosopher, theorist, and practical minded individual who truly loved the people and devoted himself to the betterment of their lives. His works continue to be very popular with Koreans to this day.

Yi Hwang:
The Shining Light of Korean Confucianism

Neo-Confucianism is a Confucian school of thought that was created by Zhu Xi of the Song dynasty during the 12th century. It is also known as the Zhu Xi School. Neo-Confucianism was a moral philosophy pertaining to social communities which centered on blood tie-based communities and the state. It was conveyed to Korea by the scholar An Hyang at the end of the Goryeo Dynasty (918 - 1392). Neo-Confucianism was later adopted as the ruling principle of the Joseon Dynasty (1392 - 1910).

Yi Hwang (1501 - 1570), whose pen-name was Toegye, has been evaluated by many as the greatest Neo-Confucian scholar to emerge after Zhu Xi. Yi devoted himself to analyzing the philosophical basis of Neo-Confucianism, and to actualizing these tenets in his everyday life. Viewing learning and practice as one, Yi regarded unapplied knowledge as useless. He consistently refused to accept any of the high ranking positions which were awarded to him by the king, preferring instead to accept his studies as his life-long friend. Always concerned about the hardships faced by the common people, Yi never allowed himself or those around him to engage in any improprieties.

His attitude toward study and life in general are vividly reflected in his 14-year long correspondence with Ki Dae-seung, a scholar 26 years his junior, over the merits of the sadan chiljeong. While Sadan refers to the innate moral qualities (humanity, righteousness, propriety, and wisdom) known as the four beginnings, chiljeong refers to the seven human feelings (joy, anger, grief, fear, love, hatred, and desire) as defined under Confucianism. Yi Hwang's willingness to accept his errors and modify his theories during his back and forth with Ki Dae-seung is clear evidence of his open-minded nature.

Koreans have always respected the genuine manner in which Yi approached his studies. This deep-seated respect is evidenced by the fact that not only was a street named after him in downtown Seoul (Toegye-ro), but his face also adorns the 1,000-won bill. In fact, whenever they stroll down Toegye-ro or use 1,000-won bills, Koreans' thoughts naturally turn to Yi and his quest for spiritual enrichment.

An Jung-geun:
The Father of the Independence Movement

Koreans regard the Japanese colonial period (1910 - 1945) as the most tragic era in the 5,000-year history of their nation. Japan began its full-scale invasion of Joseon in the aftermath of its victory in the Russo-Japanese War (1905). It forcibly usurped Joseon's sovereignty in 1905, before formally turning it into its colony in 1910.

An Jung-geun (1879 - 1910), who strived to stop the Japanese encroachment on his homeland, is widely hailed as the father of the Korean independence movement. An was born in the northwestern Korean city of Haju. Having studied Chinese classics in a seodang - private village school during his youth, An became a Catholic at the age of 16. While he increasingly focused his energy on modern Western studies, his studies were subsequently interrupted by the need to come to the rescue of the motherland.

The Korean peninsula having already fallen under the control of Japan, An fled to Vladivostok, an area where many Koreans had taken refuge. It was from there that he amassed some 300 righteous army soldiers to take part in an attack on the Japanese units stationed in the northern areas of the Korean peninsula.

Along with eleven other colleagues, An in 1909 established a secret organization known as the Danjihoe which had as its main goal the saving of the motherland. Danji literally means cutting off one's finger. As they swore to sacrifice their lives for the homeland, each member proceeded to cut off his fourth finger. Using their severed fingers, each member wrote out in blood the words 'independence for Korea (daehan dongnip)'. This blood represented much more than mere plasma, it signified the souls and patriotic mindsets of these brave individuals.

On October 26th, 1909 An stepped onto the railway platform in Harbin, Manchuria. Unable to forgive the Japanese Resident-General Ito Hirobumi, whom he blamed for having destroyed the peace of Joseon Dynasty and East Asia as a whole, An had decided to assassinate the person who he regarded as the most visible face of the enemy. In his capacity as the leader of a Korean righteous army, An arrived at the Harbin Train Station, where he lay in wait for the moment Ito stepped off the train. When that moment finally arrived, he fired a total of seven shots, one of which took the life of Ito. At the time of his arrest, An was busily screaming out for Korean independence and waving the Korean flag.

The death of An Jung-geun spawned many other An Jung-geuns. Inspired by the spirit of An Jung-geun, Koreans from all walks of life continued the fight to achieve the independence of the motherland for another 35 years.

Yu Gwan-sun: The Joan of Arc of Korea

March 1st, 1919 marks the day in which Koreans rose up as one against Japanese colonial rule and informed the world of their desire for independence. This day is now a national holiday in Korea known as 'Samiljeol'. In this regard, every Samiljeol, Koreans thoughts naturally turn to Yu Gwan-sun (1902 - 1920). A very active and passionate girl, Yu's heart was filled with the spirit of independence. Born into a Christian family in Cheonan (a city located in the central area of the Korean peninsula), she later attended Ewha Hakdang, the very first Protestant women's school in Seoul.

In November 1918, World War I came to an end. Shortly thereafter, the President of the United States Woodrow Wilson announced his support for decolonization and national self-determination. While Wilson's declaration provided hope and courage to small and weak ethnic groups that found themselves under the rule of strong powers, it electrified Koreans. The Korean sense of outrage and willingness to stand up to tyranny reached a new zenith following the death under suspicious circumstances of the 26th and last monarch of Joseon Dynasty King Gojong (r. 1863 - 1907) in January 1919.

This event proved to be the spark which Koreans needed to unite. It was under such circumstances that the March First Movement was born. Yu Gwan-sun, a high school girl at the time, organized a special independence squad with her friends from the Ewha Hakdang that participated in the March First Movement. The participation of many students in the movement caused Japan to order the closure of all schools on March 10th. Yu then returned to her hometown, where she prepared a demonstration in favor of independence. The march for independence included not only people from her hometown, but also from neighboring towns such as Mokcheon, Anseong, Jincheon, and Cheongju.

At 12:00 on April 1st, 1919 scores of people gathered at the Aunae marketplace in Byeongcheon. Once the Korean Declaration of Independence had been read, all of those in attendance broke out into a chant of "Daehan Dongnip Manse (Long live Independent Korea)!" In an instant, Japanese soldiers began to shoot into the crowd. Yu's mother and father were killed almost instantly. Yu Gwan-sun was herself sent to a Japanese military prison where she continued to advocate the independence of Korea. The victim of severe torture, Yu died in prison on October 12, 1920.

Chapter 04

Tradition, Food, Everyday Life

Hanbok / Saekdong / Dadeumijil / Kimchi / Tteok / Jeonju bibimbap / Gochujang / Doenjang and Cheonggukjang / Insam(Ginseng) / Samgyetang / Bulgogi / Naengmyeon / Jajangmyeon / Soju and Makgeoli / Onggi ware / Hanok / Chogajip / Doldam / Ondol / Dongui bogam / Taekwondo / Gangneung Danoje Festival / Yeongsan Juldarigi / Sotdae and Jangseung / Dure / Dolhareubang / Jamnyeo / Oiljang / Jeongja namu / Ssireum / Seodang / Archery / Han Seok-bong and his mother / Yutnori

Hanbok: Clothing of the Wind

The hanbok, the traditional Korean costume, developed under the influence of Buddhism, Confucianism, China and even the Mongols. While people these days wear a hanbok on special occasions and holidays, Koreans used to wear it on a daily basis.

A hanbok consists of upper and lower garments. The basic components of a hanbok are a skirt (chima) and jacket (jeogori) for women, and pants (baji) and a jacket (jeogori) for men.

The hanbok dates as far back as the Three Kingdoms Era (18 BC - 660 AD). An early type of hanbok can be seen in the 4th-6th century mural paintings found in the Goguryeo (57 BC - 668 AD) tombs uncovered in Manchuria and North Korea. Taking a look at the garments depicted in the mural paintings, we see that the upper garments (jeogori) of the men and women covered their pants and skirts respectively. The width of the pants was narrow, while the skirts were longer. In addition, the topcoat (durumagi) extended to well over the knees.

The hanbok is a beautiful article of clothing which boasts exquisitely harmonized lines and patterns. The colors of the cloth, designs, and ornaments combine to create the hanbok's refined and magnificent mood. Generally, a hanbok features two colors or more that are arranged in accordance with the concepts of yin & yang and wu hsing .

There are various kinds of hanbok. The most obvious division is that between regular and ceremonial clothes.

Ceremonial clothing can in turn be divided into hanbok for wedding ceremonies and those for ancestral rites. Although this is no longer the case, the regular clothes of the royal family were quite distinct from those of the aristocracy, which were in turn different from that of commoners. In particular, the king and queen wore various costumes, all of which were differently designed in accordance with the time, place, and characteristics of the occasions to which they would be worn.

Various fabrics can also be employed to make a hanbok. Thus, while ramie and hemp fabrics, which can be stiffly starched, were used to make summer clothes, soft, thin and refined silk was used to make spring and autumn clothes, and a warm satin fabric was usually employed when creating winter clothes.

The hanbok specifically designed for women are made in a manner which highlights the harmony between their straight and curved lines. As the train of the hanbok skirt gracefully flutters when the wind blows, the hanbok is also known as the clothing of the wind; an appellation in large part due to the aesthetic beauty of the skirt's silhouette as it flutters in the wind. Le Monde, a French newspaper, once described the hanbok as "the clothing of the wind which embraces the aesthetic beauty of concepts such as roundness, tranquility, and naturalness, while accentuating a woman's face and shoulders."

One naturally becomes more aware of the movement of his/her body when wearing a hanbok. The hanbok is more than simple clothes; rather, it is a form of clothing which embraces the Korean spirit, rites, and traditions.

One cannot discuss the hanbok without touching on the subject of ornaments. Ornaments were used to strengthen the functions and efficiency of the hanbok or simply to change its style. The higher the class one belonged to, the more splendid the ornaments utilized became.

Korean fashion designers have made efforts to internationalize the hanbok. In this regard, Lee Young-hee can be singled out as the representative example of such hanbok designers. She has focused on applying the hanbok's straight and curved lines and its designs to modern-style clothing, and on changing the traditional hanbok in order to create a new fashion style.

©Lee Young-hee

Saekdong: The Color of Korea

Koreans have long perceived colors as part of a system endowed with both social and universal meanings. In this regard, the obangsaek (five colors) can be perceived as the most famous Korean color-related notion. More to the point, obangsaek refers to the colors associated with each of the five cardinal directions (east, west, south, north and center). While blue is used to describe east, white represents west, red south, black north, and yellow the center. However, liberal combinations of the colors found in the obangsaek, or saekdong, were subsequently created.

Saekdong refers to a stripe that features many colors. For the most part, it consists of shades of green that have been combined, with the notable exception of black, with the obangsaek colors. Saekdong exudes a sensual and exceptional aesthetic beauty that is achieved through the combination of strong colors.

Saekdong reminds one of a rainbow, which in turn evokes thoughts of children's pure dreams. In this regard, clothes featuring saekdong patterns were commonly provided to children between the ages of one to seven on December 31st (lunar calendar). The princes from the royal family regularly wore saekdong durumagi (overcoats) on Buddha's birthday. The wearing of saekdong clothing

was widely perceived as a direct means of of expressing an auspicious omen. The use of the wide array of colors found in the saekdong in children's clothes was rooted in the belief that this kaleidoscope of colors could drive evil spirits away. Koreans also believed that children could ensure themselves of having long, happy, and healthy lives by wearing saekdong clothes on special occasions.

The 21st century has seen the saekdong come to be regarded as the symbol of Korean color patterns. Various saekdong designs have been employed to make modern clothes, beddings, and Korean-style wrapping paper. For its part, the uniforms worn by the crew of Asiana Airlines, as well as the logo on its aircrafts, feature novel interpretations of the saekdong pattern.

Dadeumijil: Nonverbal Performance

During the opening ceremony of the 1988 Seoul Olympics, all the lights in the Olympic Stadium were suddenly turned off and a repetitive sound started to ring out in the air. This was the sound of dadeumi (wooden clubs), whose rhythms are deeply engrained in the emotions of Koreans. It was precisely for this reason that its unique sounds were performed during this ceremony marking the opening of this global festival.

The term dadeumijil in fact refers to the act of smoothening clothing by pounding it with wooden clubs. Before the dadeumijil can however be carried out, the clothes first have to be starched and dried in the sun. The clothes are then sprayed with water and wrapped in a dry cloth. Once the water has been fully absorbed by the clothes, the latter is then laid flat on a dadeumi-dol made of granite and stepped on. The final step in this process involved the clothes being pounded with wooden clubs known as dadeumijil so as to render them smooth. Traditional clothing which had been subjected to the dadeumijil process not only looked impeccable, but also stayed clean for a long period of time and kept the heat in longer.

Although the dadeumijil was part of everyday chores, it has always been regarded by Koreans as more than just a simple labor. The pleasant yet sad sounds and repetitive rhythms emanating from these clubs constituted primitive forms of Korean music. Moreover, this process can also be regarded as having been a performance conducted by Korean women to soothe their weary minds. Thoughts of their mothers and hometowns naturally come to Koreans' minds whenever they hear the sound of the dadeumi.

These days, Koreans press their clothes using irons or by bringing them to the laundry store. However, the sound of the dadeumi continues to live on in their hearts. It was this very sound that led to the emergence of the wildly popular nonverbal performance known as 'Nanta.'

Kimchi: The Taste of 2,000 Years

Kimchi is in all likelihood the most popular of Korean foods. The term 'kimchi' literally means, "vegetables fermented in salt" in Korean. A variety of vegetables can be used to make kimchi; these include Chinese cabbage, turnips, squash, eggplants, sesame leaves, Korean lettuce, and stone leeks. Kimchi is created by adding salt, garlic, red pepper powder, ginger, anchovies or shrimp, pear juice, and chestnuts to these vegetables.

Traditionally, kimchi consisted simply of vegetables stored in salt to which a few basic spices were added. By the 1600s red chili peppers and pickled fish had become the main ingredients in kimchi. The modern era has seen pears, chestnuts and pine nuts also be added to this dish.

Kimchi is the main staple of the Korean diet and a dish that Koreans enjoy throughout their entire lives. Kimchi is widely perceived as being representative of Korean emotions and culture, and as an integral part of Koreans' identity. As such, for Koreans, kimchi represents much more than food.

The history of kimchi is also much longer than that of other foods. In the *Dongyizhuan* (Eastern Barbarians) section of the *Sanguozhi* (History of the Three Kingdoms)'s *Weishu* one finds an entry dealing with the food of Goguryeo in which it is written that the people of Goguryeo used salt when eating vegetables, and that they had excellent fermentation skills. Based on this record, we can surmise that kimchi is at least 1,500 to 2,000 years old.

As mentioned above, there are numerous types of kimchi. In general, the name given to a particular type of kimchi usually reflects that of the vegetable which serves as its main ingredient. For example, while a kimchi that features baechu (Chinese cabbage) as its main ingredient is referred to as baechu kimchi, it is known as mu kimchi when the main ingredient is mu (radish). However, there are some instances in which the name given does not reflect that of the vegetable which is used as the main ingredient, but rather the method which is used to prepare it. The following represents a more detailed explanation of the most popular types of kimchi.

Baechu kimchi: After having been cut into halves or quarters, the cabbage is then soaked and stored in salted water to be fermented along with various garnishes.

Chonggak kimchi: Once it has been soaked in salt, spices are added to altarimu (ponytail radish), which is then left to ferment.

Kkakdugi (Kimchi made of white radish which has been cut into cubes): Once the white radish has been cut into small bite-size cubes, it is then soaked in salted water, garnished with spices, and left to ferment.

In addition, one also finds various other types of cabbage and white radish kimchis, as well as variants made with different vegetables. Sesame leaf, parsley, Korean lettuce, shallots, leek, cucumber, egg-plant, and cabbage kimchi are usually considered to be the most notable types of kimchi.

Kimchi represents a central source of nutrients such as proteins, vitamins, and minerals. What's more, it acts as both an appetite stimulant and a great alkaline which facilitates digestion. It is known to help maintain intestinal health and to have an anti-bacterial effect. In addition, some of the ingredients used in kimchi such as garlic, red peppers, and ginger have a proven track record of preventing cancer and heart disease. During the recent outbreak of SARS (Severe Acute Respiratory Syndrome), Korea found itself amidst a media whirlwind when it became the only country in Asia to not report any cases of the virus, a denouement which has led many scientists to conclude that kimchi possesses a virus-resistant effect. As a result of such scientists' discovery of its beneficial effects, the popularity of kimchi is growing the world over.

Tteok: Korean-Style Bread

Tteok refers to a dish that is created by steaming whole grain flour. While rice flour is usually employed, other grains such as buckwheat, millet, and barley are also commonly used. Tteok has long been an essential part of national holidays such as the Lunar New Year and Chuseok (Korean Thanksgiving) as well as for more individual occasions such as the parties marking the passing of one hundred days since the birth of a child, birthday parties, and wedding ceremonies. As such, Koreans have regarded tteok as an important element of their celebrations.

It is unclear when Koreans first started to make tteok. However, the discovery of siru (a tool used to make tteok) amongst remains from the Bronze Age and in tombs dating from the Three Kingdoms Era (18 BC - 660), as well as its appearance on the mural paintings of Goguryeo Kingdom (18 BC - 668), have led many scholars to conclude that tteok began to be made sometime before the Three Kingdoms Era. To this end, a record pertaining to tteok has even been found in the famous compilation of ancient history known as the *Samguk sagi* (Chronicles of the Three Kingdoms).

Tteok was initially used by the upper class as part of ritual ceremonies to the heavens or ancestral ceremonies. In this regard, it was during the Goryeo Dynasty (918 - 1392) that tteok was widely introduced to the masses. The popularity of tteok amongst the masses increased in conjunction with the rise in the amount of rice produced. However, it was during the Joseon dynasty (1392 - 1910) that tteok truly enjoyed its heyday. This is evidenced by the fact that one not only finds 198 different kinds of tteok in the culinary books compiled during the Joseon era, but also 95 different ingredients with which to make tteok. The modern methods used to prepare tteok were first established during the Joseon era.

The most popular types of tteok amongst Koreans are garaetteok, songpyeon, baekseolgi, patteok, and injeolmi. Garaetteok is made of nonglutinous rice flour that is steamed and then shaped into long thin strips. In addition to being one of the dishes commonly served on the Lunar New Year it is also the main ingredient in tteokguk (traditional New Year's food). Songpyeon is a kind of tteok that is served during the ancestral ceremony held on Chuseok. Made with steamed nonglutinous rice flour that is shaped like a half-moon, it features a stuffing that consists of beans, chestnuts, sesame, and mung beans. Baekseolgi is a kind of tteok that is made by steaming the nonglutinous rice flour in a siru. Meant to denote sacredness, this pristine white colored food is usually served during parties marking the passing of one hundred days since the birth of a child, or first birthday parties. Meanwhile, patteok is a type of tteok usually prepared for use during shaman ceremonies. It consists of layers of steamed nonglutinous rice flour and red beans.

Songpyeon

Jeonju bibimbap:
A Dish that Encompasses the Principle of Nature

Located in the southwest of the Korean peninsula, Jeonju is widely perceived as the food capital of Korea. To this end, bibimbap constitutes the very essence of Jeonju's food culture. Bibimbap is a healthy dish consisting of rice mixed with gochujang (red pepper sauce), beef, and various vegetables such as bean sprouts, spinach, bracken, radish, and zucchini.

The first reference to bibimbap appears in the *Siui jeonseo*, a cookbook written in the Korean vernacular published in the late 1800s. Jeonju bibimbap has been selected as the best kind of bibimbap. Bibimbap is a great tasting food that is also high in nutritional value. In addition, it is a functional food which helps to ward off various diseases. For instance, the dietary fibers contained in the various vegetables found in Jeonju bibimbap help to lower the concentration of cholesterol in the blood; as such, it is a good tonic for those who suffer from high blood pressure. It is also effective in preventing cholelithiasis, diabetes, constipation, and obesity. Gochujang, from which the unique taste of bibimbap emanates, possess anti-carcinogenic properties and helps to ward off and even cure obesity.

Jeonju bibimbap is a dish that incorporates the theory of Eumyang ohaeng (yin-yang and wu hsing). Eumyang ohaeng is a philosophy which explains the principles of the universe and nature. In this regard, the ingredients used to make bibimbap feature five different colors which are meant to represent the five basic Asian cardinal directions: east, west, south, north, and center. Here, these directions should be understood to denote the world or nature. As such, bibimbap is a dish that incorporates the principle of nature, or more to the point of harmony and balance.

Having tried it on the plane on the way over, American pop singer Michael Jackson ate a diet that consisted mainly of bibimbap during his visit to Korea in 1998. Actor Nicholas Cage is another celebrity who fell in love with the taste of bibimbap after having sampled it during his visit to Korea. While these people may simply have thought that they were enjoying a healthy dish, what they in fact consumed was nothing less than the culture, philosophy, and spirit of Korea.

Gochujang: Spicy Tonic

There is an old saying in Korea that "A house with high-quality condiments or sauces (jang) will inevitably produce great tasting food." Thus, jang (fermented sauces or condiments) is believed by Koreans to have the power to determine the taste of food. To this end, Koreans have long attached a great importance to the task of making jang. The most common types of jang include ganjang (soy sauce), gochujang (red pepper paste), and doenjang (soybean paste).

While gochujang is used to give food a spicy taste, it is mainly used as a dipping sauce. Gochujang is a mixture of red pepper, glutinous rice, and meju powders (soybean malt) that is combined with malt, salt, and water and thereafter fermented for a certain period of time. While the savory taste of gochujang comes from the soybean-based meju; its sweetness emanates from carbohydrates such as the glutinous rice and malt. Meanwhile, its spiciness can be attributed to the red pepper powder and saline taste to the salt included therein. All of these tastes are combined together to create a unique new taste. Gochujang features not only a unique taste, but also various nutrients such as protein, fat, Vitamin B2, Vitamin C, and carotene.

Peppers were first introduced to the Korean peninsula during the Hideyoshi Invasions (1592 - 1598). Thereafter, peppers started to be used to make various foods such as kimchi, jjigae (stew), and bokeum (stir fry) dishes. Gochujang was finally created by adapting the methods used to develop doenjang (soybean paste).

Created using the tenets of the science of fermentation, gochujang is a product of outstanding quality. In fact, many Korean seniors credit their longevity to the fact that they have eaten doenjang and gochujang- based foods their entire lives. As it is made in part from fermented soybean, gochujang also contains a high concentration of protein. Furthermore, it is also known to have anti-carcinogenic properties and to inhibit the onset of obesity. Koreans have long regarded gochujang as a spicy tonic that sits on the dinner table and found a variety of ways to enjoy it.

Doenjang and Cheonggukjang: Medicinal Foods

Commonly referred to as 'meat from the garden', beans have long been regarded as a healthy food. Koreans have used beans to make such basic foods as doenjang (bean paste), ganjang (soy sauce), cheonggukjang (fast fermented bean paste), tofu, and kongnamul (bean sprout). In this regard, the traditional Korean foods known as doenjang and cheonggukjang are characterized by the fact that they exercise a positive effect on human health that is akin to that of medicine.

Doenjang is a basic staple of the Korean diet that is made from meju (soybean malt), which is in turn made from a mixture of boiled beans, salt, and clean water. The meju bricks are maintained in a warm spot (29 - 32°C) until sufficiently fermented. They are thereafter dried and stored in a place with a lot of sunlight. After drying for about five months, they then become the basis of doenjang. Koreans are fond of making guk (soup) and jjigae (stew) with doenjang.

Penicillin, which is used to cure afflictions such as pneumonia and septicemia, shares many commonalities with doenjang. While doenjang is the result of the interactions between mold, germs, and enzymes, penicillin is an antibiotic made from blue mold. Koreans have long buoyed their immune systems by eating this doenjang so similar to penicillin. Doenjang also has antidotal effects. For instance, it is known to help eliminate toxins from the body and to clean out the blood system. Because of its anti-carcinogenic properties, doenjang is also a good means of preventing cancer.

Unlike doenjang, cheonggukjang can be made in 2-3 days. Long-boiled soybeans that have been allowed to ferment at 45°C become cheonggukjang after a few days. Cheonggukjang is known to help digestion and to facilitate the elimination of toxins within the liver. It is also good for people suffering from diabetes, constipation, or obesity. Koreans now make cheonggukjang in both powder and granule form and use it as a health supplement.

Doenjang

Insam: Restorative Medicine from the Earth

The scientific name for insam is Panax Ginseng C.A. Meyer; here, Panax represents a combination of the terms pan and axos, which in turn can be taken to respectively mean 'all' and 'cure'. In other words, insam connotes a universal panacea. The term 'ginseng' is only used in connection with the scientific name for Korean insam. While in accordance with its scientific name the Chinese word ginseng was in the past usually employed to refer to insam, the Korean term has recently begun to be increasingly employed.

Insam is classified as a perennial plant. The roots of insam are pale yellow and its leaves and stems are green. Insam's red flowers usually begin to bloom in the spring some three years after planting. These green leaves and red flowers are an important component of insam's harmonious beauty. As Insam is a half-shade plant, a sunshading device should be employed to ensure that the plant enjoys the amount of shade it needs to grow.

Insam usually grows for about 180 days a year, or about 50 days more than American and Chinese ginseng. As a result, it boasts a strong yet delicate internal texture, outstanding medicinal properties, and even an exquisite aroma. As it takes six years for an insam plant to reach maturity, 6-year old insam is generally regarded as being of the utmost quality. 6-year old insam normally consists of a head, main root, 2-5 lateral roots, and dozens of fine roots. The main root is approximately 7cm long and 3cm wide. The entire insam plant is about 30cm long.

According to ancient Korean and Chinese medical documents, Korean insam helps to protect the internal organs, soothe the spirit, maintain one's vision, keep the human body lean, and to generally live longer. Korean insam was also very popular in the West. Korean insam was first introduced in the Western world in 1610. In the case of England, insam was first introduced through the East India Company. The high reputation of Korean insam in the West was soon thereafter cemented, as exemplified by the fact that it was presented to the king of France Louis XIV as a gift. In addition, one also finds references in his writings to the fact that Jean-Jacques Rousseau, the author of *Émile*, habitually took insam during his lifetime.

In ancient Chinese medical documents one finds records in which it is claimed that because of its outstanding medicinal properties, Korean insam was regarded as being the 'real' ginseng. Upon hearing of the presence in Korea of herbs which could ensure eternity, Emperor Qin Shi of the Chin dynasty (259 BC - 210 BC) dispatched his loyal subject, Xu Shi to the Land of the Morning Calm. Xu Shi visited the Geumgangsan Mountain, Jirisan Mountain, and Hallasan Mountain areas to find this so-called 'herb of eternity'. People have long believed that the herb of eternity which Emperor Qin Xi sought was in fact insam. Xu Shi left an inscription detailing his visit to Korea on a rock on the South coast of the Korean peninsula.

Insam has been used in modern medical science. Scientific research has been conducted in order to prove the ability of insam to prevent the onset of diabetes, prevent cancer, strengthen the heart function and control blood pressure, protect liver functions, strengthen the digestive function, reduce stress, strengthening brain functions, increase physical strength, counter anemia and strengthen the hematogenic function, boost the immune system, act as an anti-inflammatory, and slow down the ageing process.

The efficiency of Korean insam has its origins in the climatic and geographical conditions which prevail on the peninsula. Insam plants grow best in temperate zones that lie between the 36 - 38 parallels and which exhibit four distinct seasons, boast annual temperatures that range between 0.9-13.8℃, and where temperatures vary between 20-25℃ during the summer season. In addition, the ideal country for insam production is one which receives approximately 1,200mm of annual rainfall and only limited amounts of snow. The Korean peninsula meets all of these conditions.

©KGC

Samgyetang: Recuperative Dish Served during the Summer Season

Samgyetang, which is prepared by stuffing a young chicken with various ingredients such as ginseng, jujubes, glutinous rice, and garlic before boiling it for a long time, is widely perceived as the preeminent recuperative dish served in Korea during the summer season. Koreans are very fond of eating samgyetang during the dog days of summer. Why do Koreans have samgyetang on a hot summer day? The main reason is that samgyetang is a proverbial 'hot' food. People partake of cold beverages, ice cream, and cool fruit juice in order to overcome sweltering heat. However, the internal organs also become cold when one eats too much cold food. Traditional Korean medicine argued that coldness in the internal organs is at the origin of various kinds of diseases. Samgyetang is a food that helps to alleviate such coldness in the internal organs. Nevertheless, not everyone should eat samgyetang. Koreans have always placed great importance on eating foods that mesh with their physical constitutions. Those who have a 'hot' physical constitution, suffer from high blood pressure, or have had a stroke should in all likelihood refrain from eating samgyetang.

To make samgyetang, a young chicken is stuffed with glutinous rice, ginseng, jujubes, and garlic, with the legs of the chicken then tied up to prevent the contents from seeping out. Thereafter, water is poured into a special bowl until the chicken has been completely submerged. While the chicken is initially boiled over a high heat, the heat is subsequently turned to low once a boil has been achieved and left as such for about an hour.

Traditional Korean medicine separates foods based on whether they possess hot or cold properties. For instance, while pork, wheat flour, and cucumbers fall under the cold category, chicken, garlic, jujube, and ginseng fall are regarded as hot foods. Korea cuisine usually involves a mixture of hot and cold ingredients. Koreans do however, whenever deemed necessary, make foods that consist solely of only hot or cold ingredients. Samgyetang is a perfect example of a dish that consists solely of hot ingredients. Samgyetang, which is made using a young chicken, ginseng(which the First Qin Emperor regarded as the herb of eternal youth), garlic(which acts as a tonic), and jujubes (which are believed to protect the stomach and prevent anemia), becomes a complete food that is used to warm up the body.

Bulgogi: The Emblem of Korean Meat Dishes

Bulgogi is a seasoned dish of thinly sliced beef which is broiled over a fire. While the 'bul' in bulgogi means fire, 'gogi' means meat. Bulgogi, a dish with a history that spans some 2,000 years, was reserved for royalty during the Joseon Dynasty (1392 - 1910), when it was known as neobiani. Bulgogi, along with galbi, is widely regarded as the most representative Korean meat dishes.

Bulgogi draws its origins from the popular Goguryeo Kingdom era (37 BC- 668) dish known as maekjeok. Maekjeok was a dish which the inhabitants of Goguryeo prepared by skewering meat that had been seasoned with soy sauce and garlic and then broiling it over hot coals. Here, the term 'maek' refers to Goguryeo Kingdom itself, while 'jeok' means seasoned meat that has been broiled over a fire. Thus, maekjeok can be regarded as the name given to Goguryeo-style bulgogi. Historical documents indicate that maekjeok was also popular amongst the Chin people of China. However, Goguryeo Kingdom is widely regarded as the ancient state which exhibited the most advanced meat-eating culture during this period.

Goguryeo Kingdom was not the only entity on the Korean peninsula which was in the process of establishing the basic foundation of a state during this period. However, meat-eating culture soon began to fade away as a result of the fact that Silla Kingdom (57 BC - 935) and Baekje Kingdom (18 BC - 660 AD) adopted Buddhism as the philosophical cornerstones of their new states. In other words, the strict prohibition of the destruction of any form of life sanctioned by Buddhism caused the development of a meat-eating culture to grind to a halt.

The custom of eating meat once again rose to the surface following the so-called 'Mongol invasions'. These invasions had the effect of conveying the food culture of the nomadic Mongols, of which meat was an integral component, to the people of Goryeo Dynasty (918 - 1392). It was not long after the Mongols reintroduced meat into the Korean diet that Goguryeo's traditional meat-eating culture resurfaced in the capital area of Gaegyeong (presently Gaeseong). Over time, this culture led to the advent of the dish reserved for the royal palates of Joseon known as neobiani, before finally becoming what is commonly known as bulgogi.

Good tender meat is an important part of making tasty bulgogi. Beef tenderloin that has been scored lightly with a knife to make it tenderer should be employed, with the meat then marinated in pear juice or rice wine and sugar. It is the enzymes of the beef which cause the meat to achieve the desired degree of tenderness. Once this has been established, the marinated beef should be mixed thoroughly with a seasoning sauce consisting of soy sauce, chopped green onions and garlic, sesame salt, ginger, pepper, and sesame oil.

There are many instances in which Korean food is even more delicious when served with other ingredients. With this in mind, bulgogi is usually served with some form of ssam (wrapping) and kimchi. Ssam is the term used to connote the practice of wrapping foods such as bulgogi with vegetables such as lettuce, sesame leaves, crown daisy, or ssamjang. The taste of ssamjang is the most vital factor when it comes to the ssam. Ssamjang is a sauce made by mixing doenjang (bean paste made of fermented beans and salt) with gochujang (pepper paste made of fermented grains and pepper). Ssamjang, which is fermented, not only helps to improve the taste of bulgogi, but also people's health.

While rice can be regarded as representing the main Korean staple in terms of grain, and kimchi can be perceived as the symbol of Korean vegetables, then bulgogi can be viewed as the most representative Korean meat dish. Bulgogi, one of the dishes most beloved by Koreans, has a 2,000-year history. Therefore, eating bulgogi consists of more than partaking of a savory meat dish; it represents an opportunity to experience Korean tradition and culture.

Naengmyeon: Exquisite Flavor of Summer

Naengmyeon (literally cold noodles) is the most common noodle dish enjoyed by Koreans during the hot summer months. Naengmyeon is said to have two birthplaces: the North Korean capital city of Pyeongyang and the city of Hamheung in Hamgyeong-Do Province, North Korea. As a result, many restaurateurs in Korea have given names such as Hamheung naengmyeon or Pyeongyang naengmyeon to their establishments.

There are however obvious differences between Hamheung naengmyeon and Pyeongyang naengmyeon. The noodles used for Hamheung naengmyeon are made of locally produced potatoes, corn, and yams, and are usually thin and tough. Gochujang (red pepper paste) is then mixed in with the noodles to give it a spicy taste. Because of this mixing of ingredients, Hamheung naengmyeon is also known as bibim (mixed) naengmyeon. Hamheung is located on the East Coast of the peninsula where the cold and warm currents encounter one another. There is an abundance of marine products in the area. These are added to naengmyeon to create hoe naengmyeon.

The noodles used for Pyeongyang naengmyeon are made of buckwheat. These noodles are thicker and easier to cut than those used for Hamheung naengmyeon. This particular variant is characterized by its delightfully smooth taste. The noodles are served in an ice-cold broth. The types of broth employed include pheasant broth, bone broth, and dongchimi soup. Dongchimi is a kind of kimchi soup that is made of radish, green onion, garlic and pear served in salted water. It is a delicacy that is enjoyed cold during the winter. Koreans are very aware of the joy of eating naengmyeon served in iced dongchimi soup. As it is eaten with soup, Pyeongyang naengmyeon is also called mul naengmyeon.

The basic feature of naengmyeon is the presence of a garnish known as gomyeong (thinly sliced cucumbers, pieces of pear, boiled egg halves, and pieces of boiled beef) on top of noodles made from sweet potatoes and buckwheat. While this dish becomes mul naengmyeon when broth is added, it is referred to as bibim naengmyeon when gochujang is present. Moreover, when raw fish is added to bibim naengmyeon, it becomes known as hoe naengmyeon. Furthermore, naengmyeon can also be served in a mixture known as mul kimchi, which is made with baby radishes. In such instances it is known as yeolmu naengmyeon.

Naengmyeon is one of the shining lights of Korea's noodle culture. Whenever they seek a special taste or have no appetite, Koreans turn to naengmyeon. In many ways, naengmyeon is for Koreans what pasta is to Italians and udon to the Japanese.

Jajangmyeon: A Dish that Evokes Fond Memories

When Korean parents take their children out to eat one particular dish keeps popping up in their heads. This dish is none other than jajangmyeon, the noodle of nostalgia. For Korean parents who grew up during the 1970s, eating out with the family meant having jajangmyeon. This was a period in which the dining-out culture had yet to truly take root. Tasty and inexpensive jajangmyeon was a dish that was eaten when one had a special family occasion to celebrate. Despite the fact that lifestyles have changed and the people are now much more well off than they were then, the children of today like jajangmyeon as much as they do hamburgers and pizza.

Jajangmyeon is a dish of noodles served with a Korean-style black bean sauce to which sliced onions, potatoes, and pork are added. Many Koreans believe that jajangmyeon is in fact a Chinese dish. This reasoning is associated with the fact that it appeared in Korea along with the first wave of Chinese immigrants to the peninsula. More to the point, the opening of Jemulpo Port in 1883 resulted in the creation of a Chinese quarter in Incheon. The Chinese who lived in this area took to selling foods which could easily be eaten to the laborers at the port. One of these foods was jajangmyeon.

Although jajangmyeon was created by Chinese people, one cannot find the exact replica in China. While one can find a noodle dish which is topped with Chinese-style bean paste, this is completely different from Korean jajangmyeon. The simple fact is that the taste of Chinese-style black bean paste is completely different from that used in Korean jajangmyeon. Korean jajangmyeon has recently begun to be exported to China. As such, a Korean food dish that was originally developed by Chinese immigrants has now made its way onto Mainland China. The black bean paste used in jajangmyeon is also imported from Korea.

Jajangmyeon continues to be very popular amongst Koreans. However, there is more at work than taste when it comes to jajangmyeon. This is because every serving of jajangmyeon evokes fond memories of childhood. How can one forget the fact that jajangmyeon was a constant presence during all the wonderful events, such as eating out with one's family, graduation from elementary school, and birthday parties, that marked his/her younger days? To many Koreans, jajangmyeon is a special food that carries with it the fondest memories.

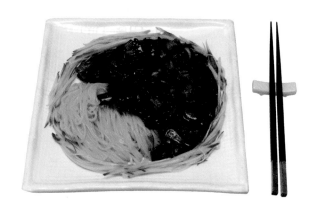

Soju and Makgeoli:
Traditional Korean Alcoholic Beverages

Alcoholic beverages have long been a regular mainstay on the Korean peninsula. For instance, the *Dongyi Zhuan* (Eastern Barbarians) section of the Chinese historical chronology known as the *Sanguozhi* (Records of Three Kingdoms) describes how Koreans enjoy drinking, singing and dancing. In other words, Koreans have always enjoyed a good party.

Makgeoli and soju are the most omnipresent examples of Korean alcoholic beverages. While makgeoli is fermented liquor, soju is created by removing the dregs from the makgeoli and distilling them. Makgeoli is made from fermenting steamed rice to which water and malt have been added. Having been consumed since the prehistoric era, makgeoli constitutes the oldest known alcoholic beverage in Korea. As the color of makgeoli is white and unclear, it is also known as takju (unclear alcohol). It contains about 6.5 - 7% alcohol.

Soju was developed by distilling makgeoli with an eye towards overcoming the famed drink's one major drawback; namely that it cannot be conserved for a long period of time. There are two different kinds of Korean soju: diluted and distilled. Diluted soju is made by fermenting and distilling rice, barley, and sweet potatoes, and then diluting it in clean water. Diluted soju has long been a favorite amongst Koreans because of its much lower cost than distilled soju. It contains about 20 - 24% alcohol.

Distilled alcohol started to be produced in Korea during the 14th century. In this regard, the tradition of distilled alcohol has been conveyed all the way down to the present. Various kinds of distilled soju, each with its own manufacturing method, taste, and flavor, have been developed in Korea's various provinces. Leading examples include the Andong soju developed in Andong, Seoul's Munbaeju, and Jeonju's Yigangju. Distilled soju, which contains 35 - 45% alcohol, possesses a more refined flavor and dignified taste than diluted soju.

Makgeoli   Soju

Onggi ware: Breathing Vessels

Korea has developed an extremely advanced ceramic culture that features such mainstays as blue and white porcelain and buncheong (powder blue-green) wares. However, Korean ceramic culture can also be regarded as being characterized by the fact that a certain form of its pottery has embarked on a slightly different path. Here we refer of course to onggi, or traditional Korean earthenware vessels that exude the essence of Korean simplicity. Various forms of pottery had been produced in Korea. During the Joseon dynasty (1392 - 1910), Koreans started to make earthenware vessels featuring glaze on the surface that came to be known as onggi. These onggi have been used to store famed Korean fermented 'slow foods' such as kimchi, ganjang (soy sauce), doenjang (bean paste), gochujang (red pepper paste), and jeotgal (fermented fish).

Onggi are known as breathing vessels. This is because small particles of sand are mixed into the soil used to produce onggi vessels. These sand particles then melt and disappear during the process of firing the vessel in a kiln, leaving behind microscopic pores on the inner wall of the onggi vessels. These microscopic pores prevent the stored foods from going bad and facilitate the fermenting process by facilitating the circulation of air and moisture.

In addition, onggi vessels contain minerals such as silicon. These minerals help improve taste and nutritional levels by causing chemical reactions with the stored foods. Furthermore, as onggi contain far infrared radiation and antioxidative properties, they are also good for storing grains. The outstanding preservative effect of onggi makes it possible to store the seeds of various grains such as rice and barley and keep them until the time comes to plant them the following year without having to worry about rotting.

The various tastes which only Koreans can create are rooted in these onggi vessels. More to the point, these onggi vessels are the reason why ganjang, doenjang or gochujang, which is contained in an onggi placed in the sunlight, or kimchi, which is generally buried in onggi crocks, are able to achieve their exquisite tastes. In this regard, some of the kimchi refrigerators recently developed in Korea have been based on the principle of onggi buried deep in the ground.

Koreans have used the soil that emanates from nature to make these seemingly natural onggi. When broken or cracked, onggi are buried in the ground where they become one with the soil. As such, they essentially return to nature. This is a virtue which plastic vessels do not possess.

Onggi features a rugged yet simple beauty. It is at once folkloric and imbibed with sentiment, while also being endowed with Koreans' traditional zest. Containing not only the wisdom of their ancestors, but their aesthetic values as well, Koreans have long displayed a profound love for these onggi.

Hanok: House Built out of Nature

Hanok is a traditional Korean-style house. The history of the hanok stretches as far back as that of Korea. Having first appeared when Koreans started to become sedentary, its history thus goes back almost 5000 years. The Korean peninsula is a place where continental are marine climates coexist with one another. To this end, the hanok is a Korean-style dwelling which was designed with the differing climate of the Korean peninsula in mind.

The hanok possesses the unique characteristic that almost all of its materials emanate from nature. The main materials used to make hanok include hwangto (Korean loess), dol (stones), namu (wood), jip (straw), pul (grass) and giwa (roof tiles). While wood is used to form the frame and pillars of the hanok; loess is used for the walls, floor, and ceiling. Meanwhile, stones are used in the under-floor and ondol (heating system) and straw and grass are employed to form the roof. The only materials which cannot be directly obtained from nature are the giwa (roof tiles). However, as these roof tiles are made out of soil there are also essentially nature-friendly.

Other characteristics of the hanok include the ondol used to heat the house and the maru (wooden floor) which functions as a form of air conditioning. Ondol is a Korean traditional heating system through which an entire room is heated by stones placed under the floor and kept warm by an agungi (furnace). This type of heating system has only been found in Korea.

Maru is a wooden floor on which people either sat or traversed on their way to another part of the home. It is usually placed about 50cm higher than the ground. The height of the maru was usually consistent with the height of a home's rooms. While the maru was usually about 1.5m wide, its length varied in accordance with the size of the house. One could only reach the rooms of a hanok after having passed through the maru. Although the maru was located at the center of the house, its presence outside of the home proper ensured that it was not heated in winter. As a result, the maru functioned as a spare room or as a corridor to play in during the hot summer season.

Based on the materials out of which the roof is crafted, the hanok can be divided into giwajip (tile-roofed houses) and chogajip (straw-thatched houses). In this regard, while the elite built their houses using roof tiles, the commoners lived in chogajip. The houses of the elite also differed from the chogajip in terms of their size. On top of their own living space, the members of the elite had houses which encompassed a separate building known as the sarangchae where visitors were received. In addition, their homes also featured another building called the haengnangchae where servants and slaves were housed. This haengnangchae was generally located near the gate.

Chogajip: The House that Nature Built

Koreans now live in houses made of concrete and bricks. These modern abodes in which the kitchens and bathrooms are established within the house proper have provided their owners with a never before felt level of convenience. However, this convenience has come at a great cost for Koreans who have found themselves having to forgo nature and simplicity. In this regard, the chogajip (straw-thatched house) can be regarded as an example of a traditional Korean dwelling that encompasses the essence of nature and simplicity.

There are two types of Korean traditional houses: hanok and chogajip. To this end, while the roof-tile (giwa) based hanok was the home of the yangban, the chogajip featuring straw-thatched roofs were the residence of the commoner. The main elements used to build these houses erected with the climate and natural environment of Korea in mind were straw, wood, and soil. The sight of the chogajip's oval shaped straw-thatched roof evokes amongst Koreans warm memories of the mountains standing majestically in back of their hometowns.

The chogajip is a nature-friendly house. It exudes a sense of simplicity that is devoid of all signs of avarice. Free of the aura of authority that characterizes the giwa-jip, the chogajip is endowed with an inherent sense of equality. The origins of chogajip can be traced back to a dugout dating from the Neolithic Age. This simplistic structure was formed by digging a hole in the ground and covering it with grass to make a roof. This type of dugout over time developed into a chogajip made of earthen walls and a straw-thatched roof.

Why did Koreans build their roofs out of straw? Rice has long been the main source of food for Koreans. However, this created a situation in which large amounts of straw remained in the fields after the harvest. The hollow nature of straw meant that the air captured inside of the straw helped to lessen the heat emanating from the sunlight during the summer months, and to prevent the house from losing warm energy during the winter.

The Hahoe Village in Andong, Gyeongbuk Province and the Nakan Eupseong Folk Village in Suncheon, Jeonnam Province are the most famous sites where one can now go and appreciate the charm of chogajip villages. Although they have long ceased to be a part of their everyday lives, Koreans continue to hold a special place in their hearts for these small simple dwellings.

Doldam: Keyword for Jejudo Island

Located on the southernmost tip of the Korean peninsula, Jejudo Island is the largest volcanic island in Korea. Blessed with breathtaking scenery, the island has become known the world over as both a resort, and the most exotic place in Korea. In 2007, UNESCO included such mainstays of Jejudo as Hallasan Mountain, Seongsan Ilchulbong (Sunrise Park), Geomun Oreum (parasitic volcano) and a few of its lava tubes on the World Heritage List.

Jejudo is a rocky island. In this regards, these rocks are the result of the melting of the lava that spewed whenever a volcanic eruption occurred on the island. Unique aspects of the culture of Jejudo, such as its dolhareubang (Grandfather Stone) and doldam (stonewall), were in turn created out of the island's hole-filled basalt.

Any introduction of Jejudo's doldam must include a few words about the ferocious winds which regularly invade the island. Jejudo Island is located along the path where the continental winds meet those emanating from the Pacific Ocean. Forced to make a living amidst this brutal wind, the people of Jejudo decided to build fences that reached all the way to the eaves of their homes in order to protect themselves from this unwanted intruder. They also commonly erected long stone fences or olle along the main roads leading into villages. What's more, they constructed stone fences around the rice paddies and dry fields in order to protect their crops from the wind. Fences known as sandam (stonewall for graveyards) were also built around graveyards so as to ward off attacks from wild animals. They made a low stone fence, or wondam (stonewall for fishing), along the shoreline. This type of fence was designed to catch the fish that had been pushed ashore by the high tide. These wondam were also referred to as a stone net.

One can find many holes in stonewalls built on Jejudo. This is because stonewalls built without any holes stand a much greater chance of collapsing under the weight of the violent winds that regularly crash down on the island. As such, these holes represent a path of sorts for the wind. A doldam erected to prevent wind erosion is called a baram geumul.

Doldam is a unique element of the scenery of Jejudo. It is also a keyword used when describing the island. The history of Jejudo and of its inhabitants' lives is imbedded in its structure. Doldam has grown to become much more than a simple element of Jejudo's scenery; in fact, it is now one of the cultural heritages that testify to the island's glory.

Ondol: A Unique Heating System

Ondol refers to a system that is used to heat an entire room using the energy created by the firing of the under-floor. Ondol is a unique scientific heating system the likes of which can only be found in Korea. Residents in the Northeast area of China also use a heating system that is based on ondol, a practice that is rooted in the fact that the area was once a part of the territory of Korean dynasties from which this tradition emanated.

The history of ondol is a very long and detailed one. Remains of gudeul (under-floor heating) have been found amongst relics dating back to the Neolithic Age. However, only parts or the contours of the walls were heated at that time, not entire rooms. The gudeul developed into a system through which the entire floor of a room could be heated approximately 1000 years ago.

The ondol system consists of an agungi (fireplace), gudeul gorae (under-floor heat passage), and gulttuk (chimney). While the agungi is essentially a fireplace, the gudeul gorae refers to the passages through which the heat and gas are disseminated throughout the under-floor; meanwhile, the gulttuk is the chimney through which the gas is expelled back out into the atmosphere. The ondol system engulfs the entire floor in a radiating heat that is reminiscent of that obtained in homes heated with wood. Moreover, as it also provides the heating and fuel needed to prepare foods outside of the summer season, the ondol is also an economical heating system.

The traditional ondol system has disappeared amidst changes wrought to the typical housing structure. Nevertheless, the method used to heat an entire room remains the same. While such rooms were in the past heated by the energy emanating from a wood fire which was passed through under-floor passages, the modern system involves the passing of hot water through pipes situated under the floor. While this modern Korean under-floor heating system has been exported to China and Central Asia, the scientific nature and efficiency of the ondol system have been recognized the world over.

Donguibogam: The Greatest Book of Oriental Medicine Ever Made

Hippocrates once said, "Let food be thy medicine and medicine be thy food." As such, he adopted the reasoning that nature was the best form of treatment for any illness. Korea also boasts a medical scholar who thought along the same lines: Heo Jun (1569 - 1618). Heo has widely been perceived as the most prominent doctor of the Joseon Dynasty era (1392 - 1910). The people of Joseon suffered from intense poverty in the aftermath of the Hideyoshi Invasions (1592 - 1598). However, despite being stricken by various illnesses, the people of Korea found themselves all but unable to obtain treatment. In addition, there was also a marked shortage of medical books. It was against this backdrop that Heo Jun began the compilation of a new medical book that was to be based on the knowledge and experience he had accumulated during his years as a doctor. The end result of this endeavor was the world famous *Donguibogam* (Exemplar of Korean Medicine).

Consisting of 25 volumes, the *Donguibogam* was effectively separated into distinct sections dealing with internal medicine, general surgery, and others miscellaneous matters related to medicine. It also included sections on the preparation of medicine and acupuncture. This incredible compilation describes the symptoms of about 2,000 diseases, as well as the effects of 1,200 kinds of medicine, the composition of 4,000 kinds of medicine, with a few hundred methods to prevent the onset of various diseases thrown in for god measure.

Koreans have long believed that various foods possess medicinal properties. In this regard, the great majority of the medicinal materials introduced in the *Donguibogam*, such as ginseng, jujubes, garlic, and beans, continue to occupy important roles within the Korean diet to this day. Heo also emphasized the fact that a good diet represented one of the key means of preventing and treating various diseases.

Considered a classic of Oriental medicine, the *Donguibogam* is a text that lays bare Koreans' perceptions of the human body, disease, and the universe. The *Donguibogam* was also published in China and Japan, where it met with much acclaim. This work thus became the first international bestseller even written by a Korean. To this end, one can still find copies of the *Donguibogam* at famous bookstores in China.

Taekwondo: A Martial Art which Involves the Training of Both Body and Mind

Taekwondo is a traditional Korean martial art whose history spans some 2,000 years. Taekwondo is more than a simple fighting sport such as wrestling and boxing; it is a spiritual exercise and a performing art which combines both stillness and motion. Furthermore, Taekwondo is an international sport which not only highlights Korean culture and thought, but one in which etiquette is regarded as being important.

Taekwondo is a combination of three words, tae, kwon and do. While tae refers to the foot techniques and kwon indicates the hand techniques, do signifies intuition or spirit. When joined together, the tae and kwon can be taken to signify the training of one's body, while do connotes the training of one's mind. Taekwon refers to the dynamic world and do the static world. Moreover, while taekwon is a metaphysical notion, do is a physical one. According to the theory of yin and yang, taekwon represents a negative energy source while do constitutes a positive source of energy. Thus, to sum up, taekwondo is at once a sport and martial art in which the body and mind, dynamic and static worlds, metaphysical and physical concepts, as well as positive and negative forces must be perfectly aligned. This is precisely the reason why taekwondo is known as a sport which demands both mental and physical discipline.

Taekwondo is often referred to a performing art which captures the Korean spirit. The splendor of this art form is contained in its dynamic and static beauty. The static beauty of taekwondo stems from the mental discipline that is required, or what we can refer to as the quest to achieve a state of stillness and calmness. This can also be referred to as the art of contemplation or meditation. Meanwhile, its dynamic beauty emanates from the movements involved. Body movements such as kicking, hitting, and thrusting connote more than simple fighting motions. Rather, these represent ways of using one's body to express one's mind, spirit, and ideas. In this regard, taekwondo is based on principles similar to those on which dance movements are founded.

The origins of taekwondo may go as far back as the prehistoric era. Unfortunately, no historical records or remains have yet been uncovered to support this claim. The first physical proof of the existence of taekwondo comes in the form of cultural remains from the Three Kingdoms Period (18 BC - 660 AD). In this regard, images of people engaging in the art of taekwondo have been uncovered in the mural paintings produced by Goguryeo during the fifth century. At that time, taekwondo was known as taekkyeon. Moreover, amongst the figures found in the Seokguram Grotto in Gyeongju, one can glimpse the faces of some of the ancient martial arts masters of Silla Kingdom(57 BC - 927 AD). Similar figures are also visible in the Bunhwangsa stone pagoda located in Gyeongju. In addition, a large number of documents pertaining to taekwondo dating from the Goryeo Dynasty (918 - 1392) and Joseon Dynasty eras (1392 -

1910) have also been found.

Taekwondo places more importance on ye (etiquette), ki (energy or spirit) and meditation than on one's strength. In this regard, yejeol (or the rules of etiquette) is widely considered to be the most important aspect of taekwondo. As such, before and after a competition, competitors bow respectfully to one another. As such, it can be said that taekwondo is a sport which begins and ends with ye (etiquette).

Taekwondo is an international sport which some 50 million non-Koreans the world over have partaken of. Taekwondo was officially recognized as an international sport following the World Taekwondo Federation (WTF)'s joining of the General Association of International Sports Federations (GAISF) in October 1975. The scope of the sport has since then expanded, as exemplified by its adoption as an official sport at the Asian Games and Goodwill Games.

However, it was its association with the Olympics which boosted Taekwondo from the status of an Asian martial art to that of a global sport. Having begun as a demonstration sport during the Seoul Olympic Games in 1988 and the Barcelona Olympic Games in 1992, Taekwondo became an official sport during the Sydney Olympic Games in 2000.

Gangneung Danoje Festival:
The Encounter between God and Human

© gangneung goverment

Located along the east coast of the Korean peninsula, Gangneung is a city that boasts a long history. The traditional image of Gangneung is that of a beautiful natural setting surrounded by mountains and the sea, as well as of traditional culture. How did Gangneung manage to maintain its unique culture amidst the mountains and sea?

As mentioned above, the people of Gangneung have been able to live their lives while overcoming the steep mountains and wavy seas. There were however also many things that had to be overcome between these mountains and seas. These included heavy rains, snow, winds and waves that posed constant threats to their existences.

To appease the raging nature and alleviate their own minds, the people worshiped mountain and sea gods and implemented ritual ceremonies. In this regard, a strong religious belief was needed to continuously hold onto hope amidst such a rugged environment. This religious belief has in turn created various cultural phenomena. One of these phenomena has been the festival known as the Gangneung Danoje Festival. Dano is the term given to a traditional summer holiday that falls on May 5th of the lunar calendar in Korea.

Detailed records related to the danoje can be found in Korean and Chinese historical documents. According to these records, danoje is rooted in the rituals to the heavens and agricultural rites of the Dongye, an ancient tribal kingdom that resided in the northeast of the Korean peninsula, or what is now Gangneung. The festival was originally called Mucheon (Worshipping the Heavens). As the Gangneung Danoje Festival originated from this Mucheon, this traditional Korean festival can be said to boast a 2,000-year history.

The Gangneung Danoje Festival has become a local festival in Gangneung City which usually lasts for one month. On the lunar calendar, it begins on April 5th and runs until May 7th. This festival originally traced back to the Dano holiday has over time become the Gangneung Danoje Festival, a happening whose innate vitality has led it to continuously accept new cultures. In May, when grains start to sprout, the people of Gangneung sought to interact with the gods by means of various rituals such as nongak (Korean folk music), nongyo (Korean traditional songs), gamyeonggeuk (mask dance-drama), minsok nori (Korean folk games), and musokje (Korean shaman ceremony). Above all, they attempted to ensure bumper crops and bountiful catches of fish. They be-

lieved that while farming would be bountiful when the gods were happy and ap-
peased, natural disasters would occur
when the gods were mad. Thus, rather
than just a festival to be simply enjoyed,
the Gangneung Danoje Festival is in fact
a traditional festival that is steeped in religious sacredness. In addition, it is also
an event that has preserved the cultural
traditions of Dano.

While stringent measures have been tak-
en to hang on to its past, the Gangneung
Danoje Festival's continued vitality has
been rooted in its ability to continuously
accept new cultures. Because of its ability to persevere for such a long period of
time without losing any of its originality
and identity, UNESCO has listed the
Gangneung Danoje Festival as a Masterpiece of the Oral and Intangible Heritage
of Humanity. This is the third Korean intangible cultural heritage to be recognized as a global cultural heritage after
the Jongmyo Jeryeak (Royal Ancestral Ritual Music) and Pansori (a genre of musical story-telling performed by a vocalist
accompanied by a drum).

©gangneung government

Yeongsan Juldarigi:
Recreation for Integration Purposes

Having originated in the village of Yeongsan situated in the county of Changnyeong in Gyeongsangnam-Do Province, the Yeongsan juldarigi (Yeongsan tug of war) is regarded as one of Korea's intangible cultural properties. More than a simple tug of war contest, this event is in fact a festival design to promote good will and unity amongst the villagers. The Yeongsan juldarigi was designated by the Cultural Heritage Administration of Korea as Important Intangible Cultural Property No. 26 in 1969. Prior to the actual commencement of the tug of war, two teams, referred to as East and West, are formed. While the East team represents the men, the West team is that of the women. This symbolism is rooted in the principle of yin and yang. The east, from which the sun rises, is the 'yang'; meanwhile, the west, where the sun sets, is the 'yin'. Therefore, while yin means women, yang denotes the men. As women are symbols of the 'earth' and 'production', people have traditionally believed that the West should emerge victorious win in order to ensure a good harvest in the upcoming year.

Before the actual tug of war contest begins, the villagers parade around to the rhythms and sounds of pungmul (Korean traditional folk music) while carrying the rope on their shoulders and shaking colorful flags. The ropes move around like a dragon. The two teams put their ropes down and square off against one another. They wave their flags toward the other team, and encourage the members of their team. The referee then gives the signal and the tug of war begins. The festive atmosphere is further reinforced by the spirited and cheerful sounds of nongakdae (farmers' bands) playing traditional music. Once the tug of war has been completed, people gather around and begin to dismantle the rope from the winning side. Koreans have long believed that placing straw taken from the roof of the winning team on their roof will bring good fortune to their families and lead to the production of sons. They also believed that if they fed the straw taken from the winning team to their cows, their cattle would be healthy, and that a good harvest could be secured when they used the manure of these cows as fertilizer. Fishermen from afar would sometimes try to purchase the rope from the winning team in order to ensure themselves a bountiful catch.

Sotdae and Jangseung: The Guardians of Villages

Jangseung

Sotdae (totem poles) and jangseung (village guardians) have long been regarded as some of the most symbolic examples of folk beliefs in Korea. Sotdae refers to a wooden or stone made bird that sits on top of a wooden pole or a stone pillar. Erected at the entrance of villages, it was designed to ensure the safety and protection of the people and good harvests. The most important aspect of this sotdae belief is the bird on top of the pole. Although most of these birds were depicted as ducks, in some regions they were rendered as crows, geese, and gulls. The majority of birds which had become the object of sotdae belief were water fowl. Koreans used to pray that these water fowl would soar into the sky and convey their wishes and dreams to the gods. They also prayed that the gods would manage all the affairs that occurred on the earth and in the water in a manner that would make it possible for the village people to enjoy good harvests and a happy life. For an agrarian society such as Korea, water was a very important element.

Meanwhile, the jangseung is a stone or wooden statue which was erected at the entrances of villages, temples, and roads. While acting as a guardian for the village, it also played the role of a border demarcating villages and of a distance chart. Eerily or amusingly rendered male and female faces were crafted on the upper part of the jangseung. A male jangseung traditionally wears a carved hat and has the characters 'Cheonha daejanggun(guardian of the heavens)' written in front of it; meanwhile, a female jangseung does not wear any hat and has the characters 'Jiha daejanggun (guardian of the earth)' rendered in front of it.

The sotdae and jangseung are regarded as leading examples of Korea's Shaman culture. Whenever an epidemic emerged in villages or natural disasters such as floods and droughts occurred, Koreans flocked to these sotdae and jangseung and implemented rituals to pray for salvation. Jangseung and sotdae were like friends who consoled Koreans' souls.

Sotdae

Dure: Custom of Sharing One's Heart

Dure refers to a traditional Korean custom of sharing labor. The traditional dure was a community that consisted of anywhere between 10 - 100 members. The custom of labor sharing first emerged when the iangbeop (method of transplanting rice seedlings) was introduced during late Joseon Dynasty. During this period, dure were used to effectively implement rice planting and weeding for the whole village during the farming season. The great majority of farmers joined the dure that had formed in their villages. In many ways, the dure was a farmers' organization that emphasized the notions of independence and equality.

The basic principle of the dure was that of helping other members. The members of a dure developed farmlands for those households within the village which did not have any access to labor. It also accumulated funds which it used to cover the costs of village events and other happenings.

The dure led to the emergence of a simple indigenous farmers' culture that was based on the spirit of helping one another. In this regard, terms such as durebap, duregi, dure pungmul, and dure ssaum can be regarded as rightful byproducts of this dure culture. While durebap refers to the meals the members shared while they worked together, dure pungmul denotes the music performances conducted by the members using traditional musical instruments such as the buk (drum), janggu (hourglass-shaped drum), and kkwaenggwari (small brass gong). Farmers planted rice seedlings and pulled out weeds as they listened to and sang along with this traditional music designed to sooth their weary from hard labors. Duregi refers to a flag on which the inscription 'farmers are the basis of the world' is written. Farmers regularly hung this flag in the places where they worked. After having completed their work, they headed back to the village while waving this flag amidst some more of the above-mentioned musical performances. Regarded as a symbol of great dignity even the yangban (the nobility) were expected to get off their horse whenever someone passed by carrying this flag.

The original characteristics of the dure have almost disappeared in the modern era characterized by the transformation of the traditional labor system into a wage-based structure. Nevertheless, the significance of the dure continues to live on. Koreans have attached the name 'dure' to movements to help the poor, cohabitation efforts, and community schools, and conducted 21st century communal campaigns rooted in its notions.

Dolhareubang: The Symbol of Jejudo Island

Jejudo Island is the biggest and most beautiful island in Korea. A volcanic island featuring natural scenery of breathtaking beauty, Jejudo has often been referred to as the Hawaii of Asia. In this regard, 90% of the surface of Jejudo Island consists of basalt, a black rock with holes that boasts a very aesthetic image. The people of Jeju have long made stone statues out of these basalt rocks that have come to be known as dolhareubang.

The term dolhareubang literally means a grandfather stone. This is because the big eyes, long stumpy nose, secretive grins, and round bellies of these structures is reminiscent of a grandfather living somewhere on Jejudo Island. According to the *Tamnaji*, a work dealing with the geography of Jejudo, the first dolhareubang was manufactured in 1754.

Dolhareubang also served as deities that protect villages and their inhabitants. Visitors are routinely met by the sight of a couple of dolhareubang standing majestically at the gate when enter-

ing a village on the Jejudo Island. Many of those who encounter these gatekeepers are overcome by a strong desire to pay their respect to these giants by bowing before them reverently. Dolhareubang are also believed to be able to ward off evil spirits. The people of Jeju used to make dolhareubang in order to protect villagers from disease and prevent the emergence of war. As such, these structures possess both shamanistic and religious functions. Women who desired to become pregnant were prone to appeal to the dolhareubang for help. There was even an old tale that all a woman who could not produce children had to do to become with child was to take pieces of a dolhareubang's nose and drink water from it. This has resulted in the presence of numerous dolhareubang with no noses on the island! Emanating from the breathtaking natural scenery of Jejudo, the dolhareubang has become emblematic of the island and its people.

Jamnyeo: The Spirit of Jejudo Island

© Jejudo provincial government

Jamnyeo is a term used to refer to the professional women divers who harvest marine products such as shellfish, abalone, and seaweed from the seas wearing no diving equipment. The topographical features of Korea, which is surrounded on three sides by water, have meant that Jamnyeo have long been a common sight on the peninsula. The term jamnyeo naturally evokes thoughts of Jejudo Island amongst Koreans. This is because although jamnyeo could be found in other areas, the great majority of them have in fact lived on Jejudo Island.

Koreans also refer to Jejudo Island as 'samdado', a term meaning an island that features many of three things; in this cases stones, wind, and women. While it is only natural to find many stones on a volcanic island, as well as wind brought in from the surrounding seas, the presence of many women is somewhat of an anomaly.

Jejudo Island has long been home to more men than women. This can be explained by the fact that many of the men who headed out to sea to fish perished after encountering heavy storms. As a result, the task of keeping the family together fell squarely on the shoulders of the women. Jejudo people were also expected to provide special tribute to the government in the form of marine products. However, as men spent most of their time out at sea, the job of harvesting these tributes also became that of women.

Thus, the women of Jejudo either had to work in the field or harvest marine products from the sea. The diving and harvesting of marine products (muljil) as such represented a struggle to move beyond poverty.

While Jeju girls started to learn how to swim at the age of seven or eight, they began to dive at the age of twelve or thirteen. By the time they had turned eighteen, they had learned the basic skills needed to dive and harvest marine products and become responsible for supporting their families. The hopes of their families rested on their shoulders. Nevertheless, their lives were filled with a mixture of joy, sorrow, and agony. There can be no doubt that the Jamnyeo played a key role in Jejudo society.

Koreans do not regard jamnyeo as simple female laborers. Rather, they perceive these women as representing the very essence of Jejudo Island. In addition, these courageous women have also become one of the island's most famous intangible cultural heritages.

Oiljang: Korea's Traditional Market

Having first emerged during the late 15th century, the oiljang (five-day market) is a Korean traditional market that continues to be popular to this day. In the past, individual markets called oiljang used to open up every fifth day in localities across the nation. This oiljang system resulted in Koreans' lifestyles coming to revolve around market day. Of course, modern Koreans no longer establish their daily lives around the oiljang system. Nevertheless, life in rural areas in many ways continues to revolve around the oiljang.

In the olden days, the entire village would spring to life when market day arrived. Market day was also a festive occasion. During this period in which transportation and communication systems had yet to develop, the marketplace served as a site where information could be exchanged. People who had nothing to purchase would nevertheless flock to the marketplace when market day came around. It was there that they could witness firsthand the joys, hopes, and dreams of life. The market was more that just a place to sell or buy things, it also boasted ssireumpan(Korean traditional wrestling contests) held and namsadangpae(itinerant performance troupes) performances. As such, on top of its obvious economic functions, the marketplace also played the role of fostering folk customs and traditional culture. These days, Koreans pay a visit to rural oiljangs whenever they desire to once again feel the tradition and human warmth come alive.

Some of the most popular regional marketplaces include the Jeju oiljang, Jeongseon oiljang, Gurye oiljang, and the Moran sijang in Seongnam. In this regard, the Gurye oiljang in Jeonnam Province is widely regarded as the one in which the traditional features of the Korean oiljang have been best maintained. Over 100 old buildings selling items such as rice, fish, vegetables, livestock and utensils sit alongside traditional medicine stores in this setting which almost looks as if it had jumped out of a historical drama or movie.

For most modern-day urban Koreans, the oiljang is little more than a pleasant memory. However, although they now shop in large-scale malls or on the Internet, the oiljang continues to live on in their hearts. This is because the oiljang continues to represent an important part of Koreans' traditional lifestyles.

Jeongja namu:
A Place of Rest and Communication

The term Jeongja namu refers to a big tree located at the entrance of a village or near houses. This big tree produces abundant leaves and branches, which in turn creates a large shaded area. The village people get together under this tree to take a rest or play games. Jeongja literally means a small pavilion where one can take a rest or engage in conversation while appreciating nature. These jeongja were usually built in places of great scenic beauty or under a big tree. The jeongja namu thus has two meanings: one is as a tree which replaces the jeongja and the other is as a tree which stands above the jeongja.

The jeongja namu is a communal space where the people of a village came come to take a rest, engage in conversation, or hold meetings about village events. It has as such served as a resting place, place to meet, as well as a space in which communication can take place.

Koreans have long perceived trees as special beings. More to the point, trees have been regarded as sacred entities which could communicate with the earth through their roots and meet the heavens through their branches. In other words, Koreans perceived trees as a messenger that could connect man to both the underground world and the heavens. The jeongja namu is intricately linked to Koreans' traditional perception of trees. To be more precise, the jeongja namu is a place where people come to meet other people, nature, and God. In other words, the jeongja namu was a universal space where man, nature and god encountered one another. However, the significance of the jeongja namu as a sacred place decreased considerably following the rapid advent of modernization and industrialization from the 1950s onwards. These days, the jeongja namu for the most part serves as a place where people can come to take a rest and communicate with others.

Ssireum: A Sport based on the Notion of Humanism

Ssireum is a traditional Korean sport in which two people wearing a belt that is wrapped around their waists and thighs compete to bring any part of their opponent's body to the ground using a series of techniques and their own brute strength. Based on the notion of humanism, ssireum is a scientific and rational sport in which little harm or injury is inflicted to one's opponent. Ssireum first originated amongst primitive societies which, because they lived before human started to use tools, had to fight against wild animals and their enemies using little more than their bodies. The first known reference to ssireum can be found in mural paintings discovered in the royal tombs of Goguryeo Kingdom (37 BC - 668 AD). Produced during the 4th century, these mural paintings vividly depict a scene of two men involved in a ssireum match under a tree as a man who appears to be a referee leans over his cane and looks on. These mural paintings make it clear that well-organized ssireum competitions were popular at that time, and that these events were considered important enough to be left behind for posterity on the mural paintings.

In agrarian society, ssireum became a form an entertainment which was carried out after various ritual ceremonies. On May 5th on the lunar calendar, or Danojeol Day, women rode swings while men engaged in ssireum on the sand and grass. On July 15th on the lunar calendar, men from each province got together to participate in a ssireum competition. On August 15th on the lunar calendar, the Chuseok (Korean Thanksgiving) holiday, representatives from each village would participate in ssireum competitions in which the honor of one's village was on the line. The man who emerged victorious after many arduous rounds of competition was granted the title of cheonha jangsa (strongest man under the heavens).

Ssireum is a Korean folk sport that is deeply engrained in the nation's 5,000-year history. Unlike the great majority of contact sports, this popular sport is a peaceful one which pursues the notions of harmony and unity.

Ssireum or Korean Wrestling, Kim
Hongdo(1745-?) Treasure No. 527,
The National Museum of Korea.

Seodang: The Roots of Korean Education

Seodang (private village school) is a traditional Korean educational institution. Koreans have long used education as a means to enhance individuals' lives and develop the state. While no records have yet been uncovered which detail the exact origin of this seodang system, Goguryeo Kingdom (37 BC- 688 AD) is known to have featured a village unit school system known as gyeongdang. In this regard, the Chinese history book *Jiutangshu* (The Old History of the Tang Dynasty) contains the following passage where this system is concerned, " The people of Goguryeo love books. As a result, they are wont to erect a big building in the center of the village, which they call gyeongdang. All the village's children, ranging from the sons of the aristocracy to those of the common class, come together in this gyeongdang to read books and learn archery."

The gyeongdang system of Goguryeo was conveyed to the Goryeo Dynasty (918-1392). The *Gaolitujing* (An Illustrated Description of Goryeo) written by Xu Jing of the Song Dynasty of China contains the following passage about education at that time, "There are two or three school buildings located in each village where the children of Goryeo go to learn from their teachers."

The educational institutions of Goryeo were subsequently passed down to Joseon Dynasty (1392 - 1910), during which time they began to be referred to as seodang. During this era, local intellectuals were fond of establishing such seodang in their hometowns. Serving as a place where the tenets of Confucianism could be learned, education within the seodang was based on the use of textbooks written in Chinese characters. This affinity can be traced back to the fact that Korea had employed Chinese characters until the Hangeul system was created in 1446.

Reading, essay writing, and calligraphy were also taught in the seodang. New students received an initiation to Chinese characters that revolved around the mastering of the *Cheonjamun* (One Thousand Character Classic). Once this task had been achieved, students then turned their attention to the study of such topics as the *Dongmong seonseup* (First Training for the Young and Ignorant) and Sohak (Elementary Learning). They were also expected to learn about Korean history and the code of conduct for children. Once this course had been completed, students then delved into the *Confucian classics* (Four books and three canonical works) so as to hone their knowledge of Confucian literature and philosophy.

In addition to its more classic form of education, the seodang also functioned as a venue in which social norms and moral standards were established. The advent of modern educational institutions from the end of the 1800s onwards marked the beginning of the gradual disappearance of the seodang. While only a few remain today, those who attend such institutions can still receive the same style of traditional education that their ancestors obtained in the past, with the notable exception that the students of today also learn Korean, English, and mathematics.

Seodang, or traditional school-
house, by Kim Hongdo (1745-?).
This painting shows young Korean
children studying during the 1700s.
Treasure No. 527.
The National Museum of Korea.

Archery: A Sport that Cultivates both Body and Spirit

A mural painting known as the Suryeopdo(Hunting painting) uncovered in the Goguryeo Kingdom (37 BC - 668 AD) era Muyong tomb depicts five warriors on horseback shooting at tigers and deer with bows. These warriors seamlessly fire their arrows while their horses are in full stride. This is evidence of the fact that Koreans have long excelled at archery.

The founder of the Goguryeo Kingdom was a man by the name of 'Ju Mong'. In this regard, the name 'Ju Mong' also carries with it the meaning of a person who excels at archery. Individuals who excel at archery have always occupied a place of predilection in the hearts of Koreans. In addition, great importance has also traditionally been placed on the bow, which is regarded as being a precious item. As it was made out of the horn of a water buffalo, the bow employed during the Goguryeo era was called gakgung. Here, 'gak' means the horn of a water buffalo, while 'gung' means bow. Gakgung is the prototype of Korean traditional bows. The gakgung not only has a long range, but absorbs the majority of the shock created after the arrow has been fired, leaving the user to experience very little of this shock.

Materials used to make gakgung include the horns and tendons of water buffaloes, bamboo trees, and fish bladder glue. Some 3,500 different processes are involved in the creation of a Korean bow. Korean bow masters continue to manufacture bows using the methods first developed by the Goguryeo people. However, despite all the scientific advancements that have been made, no glue has as of yet been found that is more efficient than fish bladder glue. These bows saved Koreans' lives and contributed to the maintenance of the country during the Yuan invasion of Korea in 1232 and the subsequent Hideyoshi Invasions (1592 - 1598). The bow was not regarded as a mere weapon. In fact, it was used as a tool with which to train both body and mind during the Joseon Dynasty era(1392 - 1910). To this end, many people continue to use bows to cultivate their bodies and minds.

Korean archers have won gold on many occasions at the Olympics. Truth be told, it is more difficult for one to make his way onto the Korean archery team than it is to win gold at the Olympics! In other words, Korea features an inordinate amount of people who excel at archery. The descendants of the master archers of Goguryeo have now spread their wings beyond Asia to win many international championships.

A Goguryeo-era mural painting depicting a hunting expedition using bows and arrows.

Han Seok-bong and His Mother:
A Prototypical Example of Love toward One's Child

Korean parents are passionate about educating their children. In this regard, one particular story provides Koreans with a good model for the education of their children: the story of the famous brush writer Han Seok-bong and his mother. This story is included in the Korean textbook used as part of the curriculum in the third grade of elementary school.

Han Seok-bong (1543 - 1605) was one of the most prestigious brush writers of the Joseon Dynasty (1392 - 1910). Han passed the civil service examination (gwageo) in 1567, and was appointed to a government post that involved the preparation of official diplomatic documents. During his days preparing various diplomatic documents, Han gained a reputation amongst foreign royal envoys for having a very poignant and beautiful writing style. This was the culmination of all the support and sacrifices made by his mother up until that point. Han, who lost his father at a young age, grew up in poverty. His mother raised him by selling tteok (Korean rice cakes). His mother used the majority of her income to purchase papers and ink sticks for her son. Han took to practicing his brush writing on big rocks and crocks in order to lessen his mother's financial burden.

The following event occurred a few years before Han passed the civil service examination. One day after having spent the last few years away from home studying under a famous teacher, Han returned home. Upon catching a glimpse of his mother who was cutting tteok, he bowed reverently before her. Then his mother suddenly turned off the lamp and said, "while I cut these tteok, why don't you write on the paper?" When the lamp was turned back on, Han noticed that while his strokes were crooked and differently sized, his mother's tteok were cut in their regular size. Han left the house once again to learn more from his teacher.

Korean parents often think of Han Seok-bong's mother while raising their children. A profound love for their children hidden beneath a rigid exterior is a virtue that most Korean parents desire to possess. As such, Han Seok-bong and his mother continue to hold a special place in the hearts of Korean parents.

Image of the calligraphy
tablet prepared by Han Seok-bong located at the Dosan Lecture Hall.

Yutnori: A Traditional Folk Game that Encompasses Dreams of Prosperity

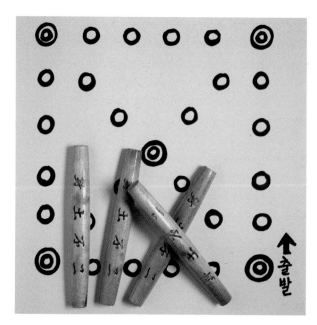

Yutnori is a traditional Korean pastime in which two teams compete against each other in a game that revolves around the throwing of four yut sticks. To play yutnori, one needs yut sticks, a yutpan (score board), and four mal (marks). While yut sticks feature one flat and one rounded side, the yutpan is a rectangular score board on which the starting point, passages and end destination have been drawn. Meanwhile, the mal (marks) are used to indicate the position of each team on the score board. Coins or wooden pieces are often used as mal.

Yutnori: essentially involves tossing the sticks in the air so as to determine how far a token can be advanced. All in all, five different combinations are possible: do, gae, geol, yut, and mo. When one stick is over (flat side up) and three sticks are up (rounded side up) this is known as do (pig). A situation in which two sticks are up and two sticks are over is called gae (dog), and one in which one stick is up and three sticks are over is known as geol (sheep). Meanwhile, a situation in which all the sticks are up is called yut (cow), and when all sticks are over it is known as mo (horse). The score is determined by counting the sticks which are over and those which are up. A do is worth one point, a gae two, a geol 3, a yut 4, and a mo 5. The team whose four mal arrive at the destination point first is crowned the winner.

The origins of yutnori can be traced back to the ancient Korean kingdom of Buyeo (which was established in modern-day Manchuria about 2,100 years ago). Buyeo placed much emphasis on the rearing of livestock such as pigs, dogs, sheep, cows, and horses. It was amidst the growing competition that emerged amongst villages to raise more livestock than their neighbors that yutnori was born. Yutnori is now one of the most beloved traditions associated with special occasions such as New Year's Day, Chuseok (Korean Thanksgiving), and village festivals.

Chapter 05

Religion,
Folk beliefs

Seon: Meditation of the Mind

Seon is a Buddhist meditational method which is designed to gather one's thoughts in one place so as to be able to contemplate and become aware of the true principles of the universe. In order to be able to engage in Seon meditation, one must first sit in the correct position and remove all rambling thoughts so as to be able to focus the mind on a specific theme. Seon carries the meaning of meditation or spiritual concentration. The origins of Seon can be traced back to efforts in India to give structure to the various meditational methods that had existed prior to Buddhism and adding Buddhist notions.

Roughly speaking, two kinds of Seon can be identified: one is the Seon associated with Hinayana Buddhism and the other with Mahayana Buddhism. Hinayana, which literally translates as 'lesser vehicle', for the most part focused on the individual enlightenment of monks. Beginning some 100 years after the death of Sakyamuni, Hinayana Buddhism constituted the main center of Buddhism for several hundreds years. Meanwhile, Mahayana, or greater vehicle, perceived monks' attempts to achieve the state of enlightenment as being carried out in conjunction with those to have laymen achieve a similar state. Having blossomed in China from the 6th century onwards, Mahayana Buddhism was then conveyed to Korea. It was thereafter introduced in Japan during the 10th century where it came to be known as Zen.

During the process of being transmitted from China to Korea, Seon developed into a Buddhist sect known as Seon Buddhism. Seon Buddhism is a form of Buddhism that revolves around meditation and contemplation (chwaseon). Korea is widely regarded as the main center of Seon Buddhism. In this regard, China has kept a natural distance from Seon Buddhism since becoming a socialist country during the mid-20th century. For its part, Japan is regarded as having deviated from the essence of Seon by creating differing levels of enlightenment. Much like a company worker gets promoted; a monk or private individual in Japan also achieves a higher rank once he becomes able to meditate for longer periods of time. This focus on the quantity of meditation rather than the quality thereof can be construed as a distortion of the essence of Seon.

Mireuk: The Messiah of Koreans

Buddhists believe that the Mireuk (Maitreya) is a bodhisattva who will one day return to our world as the rightful successor of the Sakyamuni Buddha. Meant to symbolize the advent of a new world, the Mireuk is in many ways reminiscent of the Christian Messiah. The so-called Mireuk belief first began to spread throughout Korea during the Three Kingdoms Era (57 BC- 660 AD). The introduction of Buddhism to Korea saw this Mireuk belief be creatively reinterpreted from the standpoint of the minjung (people). The Mireuk effectively became a symbol of hope for Koreans. Whenever war emerged, the country was in chaos, or natural disasters such as epidemics and bad harvests occurred, Koreans patiently waited for the arrival of the Mireuk who would make their lives happier. Although the Mireuk never really emerged to save them, this belief allowed them to keep their faith and hope alive.

The Mireuk has in many ways always been a part of Koreans' everyday lives. One can find effigies of this divine being situated at the entrance of villages, on the side of roads, or even in the deepest mountains. The practice of placing a Mireuk near one's village can be understood as a sign of the fact that the Mireuk belief was perceived as that of the minjung. This resulted in the Mireuk statues being created out of big rocks in a rough and unrefined manner. The Mireuk has always kept watch over Koreans' lives. The folk belief Mireuk was over time incorporated into the minjung's life, where it became a power for reform during periods of upheaval.

In Korea, one can encounter villages named mireuk-li or mireuk-gol, mountains named mireuk-san, and temples called mireuk-sa. All of these names were given with the hope that Korea would someday become the land of the Mireuk.

Hyo: The Moral Duty of Respecting One's Parents

Hyo (filial piety) refers to the granting of respect and the taking care of one's parents. Hyo, which was based on Confucian norms, has long been regarded as one of the most important virtues in Korea. This notion of hyo is closely related to the patriarchal system. The culture of recognizing the authority of parents and honoring them was naturally formed as part of the emergence of a family system in which the head of the household held sway over the family. Hyo was the result of the concretization of the culture of respecting one's parents into ultimate social norm and moral virtue.

There are in essence two types of hyo: one involves the expression of filial piety for one's living parents and the other a similar expression of respect for one's deceased parents. Supporting one's living parents through the provision of material goods and labor, as well as spiritual respect, is regarded as some of the measures which should be taken to express filial piety for living parents. Meanwhile, the conduct of ancestral rituals for the souls of one's deceased parents can be regarded as the most common act of filial piety conducted by children whose parents have passed away.

The hyo culture began to take root in Korea from very early onwards, with ancient educational institutions focusing on instilling students with the merits of this notion. To this end, one can find scores of ancient historical documents that detail acts of filial piety conducted by sons and daughters. Large volumes filled with stories of filial daughters and sons were also published during the Goryeo Dynasty (918-1392) and Joseon Dynasty (1392-1910) eras.

The patriarchal system is no longer as all-encompassing as it once was in Korea. In this regard, although the hyo culture has also been altered, the fundamental concept has remained unchanged. Koreas still respect their parents and conduct ancestral ceremonies to honor them after their passage. The Korean language is one which is replete with honorific terms. This practice also originated from Korea's hyo culture that regards respect for one's parents and other adults as a cardinal virtue.

A scene depicting the implementation of an ancestral ritual ceremony.

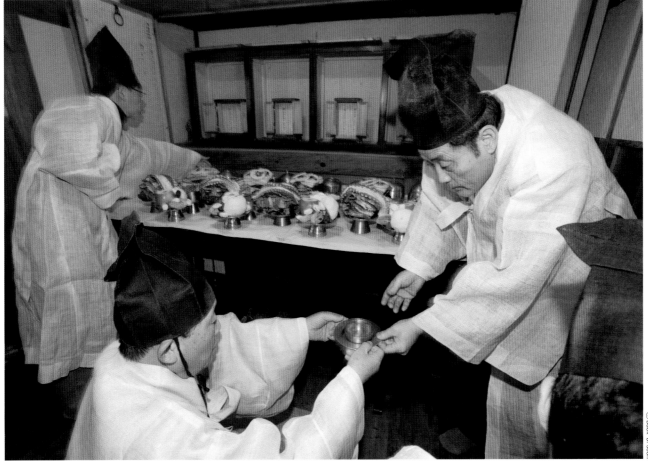

©Baek Ji-soon

Seonbi: The Intellectuals of Korea

The seonbi were individuals whose scholarly attainments were surpassed only by their honorable personalities. They were in essence the precursor of the modern-day intellectuals. These individuals incessantly strove to further expand their knowledge, an exercise which they perceived as the key to rounding out their personalities. They also possessed a strong sense of integrity and a thirst for justice. Furthermore, they went to great lengths to ensure that their actions reflected their words. These intellectuals were as such the moral leaders of the day, or an elite with a conscious.

For a very long period of time, the seonbi have encompassed the very spirit of Korea. Having first emerged during the late period of Goryeo Dynasty (918-1392), the seonbi became the main actors in Korean history during the Joseon Dynasty (1392-1910). The seonbi's consciousness of themselves as a distinct class was enhanced when Confucianism was introduced into Korea by China's Yuan dynasty during the late period of Goryeo. Joseon's adoption of Confucianism as the ruling ideology of its new state saw the seonbi emerge as the class responsible for actualizing the Confucian ideology. Possessing intricate knowledge of Confucianism, the seonbi class pursued communal rather than individual interests, and refused to negotiate with the injustice.

The seonbi sought to incorporate the Confucian ideology and values into their bodies and spirits through such practices as reading and moral cultivation. They dreamt of the day where the tenets of Confucianism would move beyond the realm of theory and be put into practice. What they sought to achieve through Confucianism was not material wealth, but rather an upright spirit and benevolent mind.

The strength of seonbi spirit emanated from their criticism and active opposition to all things which they regarded as illegal, non-humanitarian, or contrary to the notions of freedom, and peace. The tradition of the seonbi spirit has resurfaced whenever the country has found itself in crisis. The seonbi spirit was front and center during the Japanese colonial era as the people sought to restore Korean independence, as well as in the democratization movement that labored endlessly from liberation in 1945 to the 1980s. These efforts helped Koreans achieve democratization in an unprecedentedly short period of time. Having effectively been brought into line with periodic changes, the seonbi spirit continues to radiate throughout Korean society today.

Portrait of Kim Si-seup (1435-1493):
a preeminent Joseon-era seonbi.

Jongmyo Jerye and the Jongmyo Jeryeak:
Ritual Ceremony to Invoke the Spirits of the Royal Ancestors

Jongmyo is a Joseon Dynasty (1392 - 1910) era Confucian shrine in which the memorial tablets for the dynasty's kings and queens are preserved. Koreans regard the Jongmyo shrine as being important not only from an architectural standpoint, but also from a spiritual perspective. This sentiment is in large part the result of the graceful and dignified Jongmyo Jerye and Jongmyo Jeryeak which are performed within this architectural space.

Praising the cultural, social, artistic, scientific, and technological importance of Jongmyo, which it regarded as the standard for royal Confucian shrines, UNESCO included the Jongmyo Shrine on the World Cultural Heritage list in December 1995. Jongmyo Jerye, a ceremony performed in accordance with Confucian procedures, was a solemn and reverent national ritual hosted by the king. Designed to highlight filial piety, which was regarded as one of the basic virtues under Confucianism, the ritual ceremony took on the attributes of a national ritual performed in a solemn atmosphere. The performance of Jongmyo Jerye consists of three distinct sections: the welcoming of the spirits and gods, the performance of the actual ritual ceremony for the gods, and the ceremony to send off the gods.

While the ritual is being conducted, temperate music, song, and dance, which are collectively referred to as the Jongmyo Jeryeak, are performed to create a solemn atmosphere. In this particular style of music, the singers and dancers engage in their own performances while accompanying the music created by the royal orchestra using instruments native to Korea. With its dignified rhythms and tunes, the Jongmyo Jeryeak carried out the role of imploring the heavens, moving the earth, invoking the spirits of former kings, and praising the achievements of royal ancestors.

Koreans have long believed that while the Jongmyo Shrine represents the human body, the Jongmyo Jeryeak is in fact the symbol of the human spirit. The enhanced artistic and architectural beauty of the Confucian shrine and the integrated arts performed to console the spirits contained in the shrine, have harmoniously melded together to create a unique culture and spiritual values.

Much to Koreans delight, the Jongmyo Jerye is still performed once a year at the Jongmyo Shrine. On the first Sunday of May, the descendants of the royal family perform traditional rites which have now been conducted for in excess of 500 years.

Praising its cultural and spiritual significance, UNESCO made the decision on May 18, 2001 to include the Jongmyo Jerye and Jongmyo Jeryeak on the World Intangible Cultural Heritage list.

Gut: The Root of Folk Belief

Gut is the name given to Korean traditional rituals in which a shaman prays to the heavens for the people's continued happiness and health. Viewed solely from a religious standpoint, gut is a shamanistic ritual performed by a shaman, or mudang. However, the important roles played by music, singing, dancing and acting means that the gut can also be perceived as a performing art

In ancient times, gut was a state-led event that involved praying for the continued prosperity of the nation. Over time, it also began to gradually gain traction amongst the public as well. While gut was also carried out by the royal family until the Joseon dynasty (1392 - 1910), it became a uniquely private phenomenon from the 20th century onwards.

Gut consists of three processes: the evoking of the gods, offering of sacrifices and prayers, and the act of seeing the gods off. Each process features a wide variety of dances, songs, and percussion music. Gut can be broken down into maeul gut and mudang gut. Maeul gut is carried out by the community on the occasion of the Lunar New Year, during the planting season, or at the time of the harvesting of the crops. The main objective behind the holding of this particular gut is that of praying for a good harvest and the continued safety of the village. Maeul gut not only promoted the unity of the community, but also allowed the villagers to temporarily escape the doldrums of everyday life. It was also the most anticipated event within the community and was regarded as a village festival. One of the most famous aspects of the maeul gut is the seonang gut held to worship the village guardian (seonang).

Meanwhile, the mudang gut is conducted by a shaman. The mudang is believed to play the role of the intermediary between the gods and man. Their role is similar to that played by priests and ministers in the Catholic and Protestant religions. There are two kinds of mudang: one is the gangsin mudang, who is possessed by a god or spirit during the ritual, and the other is the seseup mudang, who, despite the fact that she is not animated by a god or spirit, nevertheless inherits the right to perform the shaman rituals because someone in her family was a gangsin mudang. Mudang gut involves rituals for both the living and the dead. The most common shaman ritual for the living is the yongwang gut performed to pray for continued safety and a good catch while out on the high seas. For their part, the ogu gut and ssitgim gut are representative shaman rituals for the deceased. These are conducted to pray that the deceased will enjoy eternal life in heaven, and forget all the pains and sadness he or she incurred during his or her lifetime.

Seonangdang: Altar for the Village Tutelary Deity

Seonangdang is a sacred place where the village's tutelary deity is worshipped. The term seonang refers to the tutelary deity who acts as the protector of a village. Meanwhile, although dang was a term which originally meant a house, it has now come to mean a place or site. Seonang belief is one of the cornerstones of Korean traditional shamanism. There are two types of seonangdang : one is a circular-cone shaped stone pile and the other is a small roof tiled house. The circular-cone shaped stone pile has a longer history, and is also more common than the roof tiled house-type.

A tall tree, known as dangsan namu, is usually located next to the seonangdang. Here, dangsan refers to the mountain or hill in which the village tutelary deity resides. The tree is usually accompanied by a jangseung (totem pole) made of rock or wood. These seonangdang are usually located at the entrance of a village, near the summit of a path, or on the side of the main road. Geumjul (golden ropes) are usually hung around the seonangdang.

While the exact period in which the seonangdang first emerged remain unclear, it is widely believed that the custom of carrying out ritual ceremonies under a birch tree en vogue during the Gojoseon (2333 BC- 108 BC) era has its origin in the seonang belief. The first historical record relating to the Korean seonang belief appears during the reign of King Munjong (1019 - 1083) of the Goryeo Dynasty (918 - 1392). According to this record, seonangdang were established in various villages in each province. These served as the sites in which the rituals to the seonang god were conducted in order to pray for the prosperity of the village and country, good harvests and fishing, good health, as well as the continued happiness of the family. These ceremonies were referred to as seonangje (seonang ritual).

The roof tiled house-type of seonangdang first began to emerge during the Joseon Dynasty (1392 - 1910). In such instances, a small roof-tiled house was built, and an altar was established inside of the house. Images of a seonang god with human features were drawn on the walls. The seonangdang played host not only ritual ceremonies, but to gut (shaman rituals) as well. In this regard, gut rituals continue to this day to be performed on an annual basis in a famous seonangdang. As such, the seonangdang, much like family rituals and gut, began as a folk belief, but over time developed into an inherent aspect of Korean traditional folk culture.

Geumjul: The Rope of Prohibition

Geumjul is a term which refers to a golden rope that is hung at the entrance of a sacred place. It has traditionally been hung when a baby is born, to drive away evil spirits, or when women make basic foods and condiments (jang). The shamanistic practice of using geumjul as a means to drive away evil spirits or to pray for cleanness has very deep roots in Korea. While it was widely carried out amongst the general public until the 1970s, it is now only used during special occasions.

Although different terms were used to refer to geumjul in different provinces, such as in-jul, the basic meaning was the same everywhere. The rope was made of cloth or straw and intertwined with red peppers, charcoal, and pine branches. Others items such as paper and various colored cloth were also hung.

Geumjul are made using methods which differ from the ones employed to create other kinds of ropes. In this regard, while rightward spirals are employed to make regular ropes, geumjul are made by twisting the straw while making leftward spirals. This unique method is based on the long-held folk belief that evil spir-

its hate anything associated with the left.

The materials intertwined with the geumjul differed depending on the occasion. For instance, while red peppers and charcoal were hung on the geumjul when a boy was born, the birth of a girl was celebrated with pine branches and charcoal. Red peppers were used to symbolize manhood. Moreover, Koreans believed that the color red drove evil spirits away. Meanwhile, charcoal prevents oxidation and corruption, removes bad odors, and has a revitalization effect. Koreans hoped that the functions of charcoal would prevent the advent of evil spirits and diseases. As such, charcoal represents cleanness. For their part, pine branches represent vitality and chastity.

Geumjul were also hung around the jangdok (a jar used to store basic foods and condiments) after basic foods and condiments (jang) were made. Moreover, it was also hung around the dang-namu (guardian tree) and the seonangdang (altar for village tutelary deity). Geumjul can also be found in Mongolia and Japan, where they also carry a similar meaning.

Dokkaebi: The Power to Drive away Evil Spirits

Dokkaebi is a mythical being that is usually depicted as a humorous yet grotesque looking goblin possessing extraordinary powers and magical talents. While Koreans are afraid of the dokkaebi, they simultaneously feel a sense of kinship with them. However, every Korean also knows that there is no such thing as a dokkaebi. If one were to ask where this dokkaebi lives, the best answer he could expect to receive is that it lives in the hearts of Koreans.

Why did Koreans feel the need to create dokkaebi in the first place? Although mankind has received many things from nature, it has always feared nature's ability to unleash such evils as heavy storms, thunder, and various forms of natural disasters. As such, mankind needed a guardian deity to protect them and drive away evil spirits. This was how the dokkaebi was born.

For Koreans, the dokkaebi represents a simplistic belief. The great majority of Koreans regarded the dokkaebi as a friendly naive being that at once also possessed mysterious powers. Believing that the dokkaebi could drive away evil spirits, Koreans were wont to carve dokkaebi into their architectural pieces. In this regard, dokkaebi designs can still be found adorning the walls of Korean temples, houses, and the roof tiles and bricks of palaces. Many stories related to dokkaebi have been conveyed all the way down to the present. Nowadays, there are very few people who actually believe that the dokkaebi can ensure happiness. Nevertheless, in all likelihood to stimulate their imaginations and emotions, the dokkaebi continues to be a steady fixture in children's storybooks. The dokkaebi can as such be regarded as an old friend of Koreans.

Chapter 06

Cultural Heritages, Arts

Hangeul / Hanji / Joseon wangjo sillok / Tripitaka Koreana / Jikji / Mural Paintings / Contemplative Bodhisattva / Seosan Maesamjonbul / Celadon (porcelain) / Baekja (white porcelain) / Buncheong Ware / Maksabal / Pungmulgut / Talchum / Pansori / Arirang / Geomungo / Daegeum /Chunhyangjeon

Hangeul: The Alphabet of Love

Hangeul was invented in 1443 by King Sejong, who was the fourth king of the Joseon Dynasty (1392 - 1910). According to the records compiled during the 25th year of King Sejong (1443) found in the *Joseon wangjosillok* (Annals of the Joseon Dynasty), King Sejong invented a new writing system that featured 28 letters which he called Hunminjeongeum. This writing system is now known as Hangeul.

There was a special reason why Hunminjeongeum, which means the proper language for the instruction of the people, was selected as the name of this new writing system. While Korea had long had its own language, it did not prior to the invention of Hangeul by King Sejong have its own writing system. As a result, Koreans had up until that point utilized the Chinese writing system. Aware of this situation, King Sejong set out to analyze the contemporary state of Korean phonology and to create a new alphabet system based on the proper language for the instruction of the people which he called Hunminjeongeum.

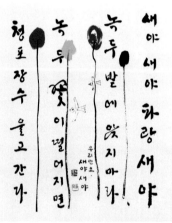

Hangeul is the only writing system whose purpose, origins, and even the identity of its creator are well known. There are over 3,000 languages in the world, and of these, only 100 feature written communication systems. However, as mentioned above Hangeul is the only writing system in the world for which we can pinpoint with exactitude the period in which it was created, the identity of its creator, and its founding principles. As can be seen from the background of this amazing writing system, Hangeul is the alphabet of love, the love which a king had for his people, whose hardships he wanted to ease.

Hangeul is a uniquely scientific writing system which nevertheless features remarkably simple principles. While Hangeul originally consisted of 28 phonemic letters, only 24, 14 consonants and 10 vowels, are now utilized. In an article published in June 1994, the science magazine, *Discovery* stressed that, "Hangeul, the Korean writing system, is a unique and ultrarational writing system whose efficiency is exemplified by the simplicity with which syllables can be combined. The simplicity and superior nature of Hangeul have helped to keep Korean illiteracy rates amongst the lowest in the world."

Pearl S. Buck, a famous American author, once said that Hangeul was the simplest yet most outstanding writing system in the world. In addition, in their textbook for university students published in the 1960s E.O. Reischauer, a professor at Harvard University, and J.K Fairbank praised the excellence of Hangeul as follows:

Cover of magazines published by
the Korean Language Society (left)
Korean traditional paper on which the Yongbieocheonga,
a Korean poem written during the 15th century, is inscribed.(below)

"Hangeul is in all likelihood the most scientific of all writing systems presently used in the world." Furthermore, Frits Vos, a Dutch linguist, once said during a seminar hosted in the United States in 1963 that Koreans had invented the best alphabet in the world.

In his book entitled *Writing Systems* (1985) Geoffrey Sampson, the British linguist who established this new category of writing known as the featural writing system, dealt with Hangeul in a separate chapter. In this chapter, Sampson argued that, "The history and theories of global writing systems have been raised to a new level with the advent of Hangeul." In addition, Hangeul ranked first in a survey of all the writing systems in the world conducted by Oxford University, a survey that was based on such factors as scientific features, rationality, and uniqueness.

As mentioned above, the *Hunminjeoneum* was included on UNESCO's Memory of the World Register in 1997. Furthermore, UNESCO has also established the King Sejong Literacy Prizes which is awarded to those individuals or groups who have made a significant contribution to the eradication of illiteracy.

Hanji: Korean Paper

In March 2005, a hanji festival was held in Paris' Bois de Boulogne Park. The famous French park came alive with lanterns shaped like tigers, jangseung (totem poles), and carps that had been made out of the traditional Korean paper known as hanji. While the citizens of Paris disappointingly thought that a sudden rain storm would result in the event being curtailed earlier than expected, light continued to emanate from these regal lanterns. Soon, the citizens of Paris found themselves even more attracted by the elegant ambiance and strong qualities exhibited by these lanterns. Amazed at this wondrous Korean paper's ability to transform itself, they went on to take in a hanji fashion show and various art exhibitions.

Paper was first introduced in Korea during the 3-4th centuries. Thereafter, using the elements at their disposal, Koreans began to develop their own paper. This eventually came to be called hanji, or the paper of Korea. Hanji is made by boiling and crushing mulberry bark. Koreans were subsequently able to create various colors of paper by dyeing these hanji with natural pigments.

Hanji was a part of Koreans' everyday lives. They used it to keep documentary records and as paper for sliding doors. The use of hanji as paper for sliding doors was motivated by its excellent heat preservation properties, and by its ability to prevent wind and moisture from seeping through. In addition, they also used hanji to manufacture basic necessities such as furniture, small drawers, and plates.

Paper has played a pivotal role in helping mankind to transmit knowledge and in the formation of a culture that places great value on the documentation of events. Koreans are very proud of hanji, a paper so strong that it is capable of remaining intact for more than 1,000 years. In this regard, Korea boasts the oldest work ever printed on a woodblock printing press: *Mugujeonggwang daedaranigyeong* (Great Dharani Sutra of Immaculate and Pure Light). Listed as National Treasure No. 126, this priceless artifact was printed on hanji some 1,200 years ago. The ability to behold this Buddhist masterpiece in the 21st century can be explained by the very fact that it was rendered on hanji, a form of paper stronger than silk.

Joseon Wangjosillok:
The Lengthiest Historical Record in the World

The Sejongsillok

The Joseon Wangjosillok (Annals of the Joseon Dynasty) constitutes a compilation of the annual records of the rulers of the Joseon Dynasty (1392 - 1910). In its pages, one finds records arranged in a sequential manner (year/month/day). Detailing 472 years of history, or from King Taejo's founding of Joseon in 1392 to 1863 in a sequential manner. These records are believed to form the most detailed records ever compiled by a single dynasty. They represent precious historical records that shed some much needed light on a wide range of fields such as politics, diplomacy, military, economics, transportation, customs, religion, astronomy, geography, music, science, natural disasters, and astronomical phenomena during the Joseon dynasty.

Comprising of 1,893 volumes and 888 books, the Annals of the Joseon Dynasty have been designated as National Treasure No. 151. There are an estimated 64 million characters included in the annals. The in-depth nature of the Annals of the Joseon Dynasty is evidenced by the fact that although the Annals of the Ming dynasty of China consist of 2,964 volumes, they only involve an estimated 16 million characters. These annals encompass records relating to a plethora of subjects ranging from politics and music to the daily lives of kings and the low-born class. Furthermore, the inclusion of detailed sections relating to diplomatic relations with other countries in the East Asian region such as China, Japan, and Mongolia has resulted in the Annals of the Joseon Dynasty being used as basic materials with which to study the history of East Asian relations during the middle and modern eras. Because of its status as a significant world documentary heritage, the Annals of the Joseon Dynasty have also been registered by UNESCO as a Memory of the World.

The compilation of the annals of a king's reign began following his death and the coronation of his successor. In this regard, the office in charge of the general affairs related to the compilation of annals was known as the Chunchugwan (Office for Annals Compilation). While the annals were initially written by hand during the early period of Joseon, they began from 1472, or from the onset of the compilation of the Sejongsillok (Annals of King Sejong) to be printed using movable metal type. At that time, Joseon possessed the most-advanced printing technology in the world, having inherited it from Goryeo Dynasty (918-1392), the first nation ever to develop moveable metal-type printing.

Joseon Dynasty established four separate repositories to store copies of important historical records such as the Annals. This storage method made it possible, despite a series of wars on the peninsula, for the Annals to be maintained intact all the way down to the present.

The task of compiling historical records in an objective manner, that is without acquiescing to the whims of those holding the reigns of power, was never an easy one under a monarchy system. Therefore, historiographers literally took their lives into their own hands when they accepted the mission of recording events for posterity. Nobody was allowed to read the Annals, not even the king. Any king who attempted to read the Annals would be stopped in his tracks by officials and historiographers willing to risk their lives to protect the truths contained on its pages. Although a king could exercise absolute power during his lifetime, he nevertheless had to be weary of the historical judgment that would be passed on him after his death via these permanent records. These fears in many ways functioned to restrain the royal power. The Annals can in this regard be perceived as the fruit of the Confucian-based principle of rule by civil officials. This fruit in turn resulted in our ability to enjoy vivid unbiased depictions of Joseon hundred of years after the events first unfolded.

© Kyujanggak

The Taejosillok

Tripitaka Koreana: Buddhist Scriptures

The Tripitaka Koreana (National Treasure No. 32) has long been housed in Haeinsa Temple located in Hapcheon, Gyeongsangnam-Do Province. Due to the high number of printing plates involved, it is also known in Korean as the *Palman Daejanggyeong* (Eighty-thousand Tripitakas). In this regard, the Tripitaka Koreana represents the most precise and complete Buddhist scriptures remaining in the world. Produced during the Goryeo Dynasty (918 - 1392) over a period of 16 years (1236 - 1251), the Tripitaka Koreana was initially intended to serve as a rallying cry for the people of Goryeo to rise up and use the power of Buddhism as a tool with which to repel the invading Mongols and restore stability to a deeply fractured society.

The process of manufacturing woodcut printing blocks was a very complex one. The printing blocks were made of birches that had been submersed under the sea for a period of three years in order to prevent decay or the trees being eaten by worms after timbering. These birches were then cut into 70cm wide, 24cm long, and 3.6cm thick blocks. Thereafter, these newly crafted blocks were boiled in salted water and dried in the sun. Once the wooden blocks had been completed, 644 characters were then engraved on each side. All in all, the Tripitaka Koreana features a total of 52 million characters of text. While both ends of each printing block were fixed with square bars to prevent unnecessary twisting, the surface was coated with lacquer to ensure that decomposition did not take place. The last steps in the completion of these wooden printing blocks involved adorning the four corners with cooper plate.

The Tripitaka Koreana is preserved in Haeinsa Temple's Janggyeonggak building. Miraculously, these wooden printing blocks have avoided all forms of damage for some 800 years. The building in which they are stored was erected using techniques that ensured that moisture would not arise from the ground, while also putting in place a good ventilation system that took into consideration the scale and direction of the wind present during each season. The tremendous value of the Tripitaka Koreana and scientific technology behind the building of the Janggyeonggak was recognized by UNESCO in 1995 when the latter included them both on its World Cultural Heritage list.

Jikji: The World's Oldest Work Produced Using a Movable Metal Type Printing Press

Koreans of the 21st century take great pride in the fact that their ancestors from the Goryeo Dynasty era (918 - 1392) developed cutting-edge woodblock printing techniques. Printing represents a very important element when it comes to the development of culture within human society. In this regard, although this particular tome is no longer available, Goryeo produced the *Sangjeong gogeum yemun* (Book on National Ceremonies and Procedures) using a moveable metal type printing press in 1234, or 200 years before such technology appeared in the Western world. Moreover, Korea also produced the oldest remaining work in the world produced using a moveable metal type printing press: the *Jikji* (*Jikji simche yojeol*, Anthology of Great Buddhist Priests' Zen Teachings).

Compiled by the monk Baekun Hwasang (1289-1374), the *Jikji* contains the teachings of both Buddha and other great monks, as well as the essentials of Zen Buddhism. In 1377, or three years after Baekun's death, his disciples at Heongdeoksa Temple in the city of Cheongju in Chungbuk Province decided to print this book using movable metal type. Although the *Jikji* originally consisted of two volumes, only the second volume, which is currently housed in the National Library of France in Paris, now remains.

The signing of the Korea-France Treaty in 1886 resulted in Collin de Plancy becoming the first French consul ever dispatched to Korea. During his stay in Korea, he amassed a collection of valuable works that included the *Jikji*. The very existence of this book first came to light when it was displayed in Paris during UNESCO's "International Book Year" in 1972. The *Jikji* was subsequently included on UNESCO's World Documentary Heritage list in 2001.

The appearance of the *Jikji* printed on a moveable metal type printing press more than 70 years before the appearance of the *Gutenberg Bible* in 1455 is proof positive of the fact that the Korean nation has long possessed great printing skills. Koreans now long for the day that the *Jikji*, which constitutes a precious treasure encompassing our ancestors' creativity and souls, is finally returned to Korea.

Mural Paintings: Mirrors Reflecting the Very Soul of Goguryeo Kingdom

Goguryeo (37 BC - 668 AD) was a kingdom that boasted both strong national power and a high level of artistic ability. Believing their kingdom to be the center of the universe, Goguryeo held sway over an area that stretched over the Korean peninsula and what is now the Northeast region of China. Goguryeo Kingdom is above all famous for the mural paintings depicting the daily lives of the people of Goguryeo crafted in the tombs of kings and members of the aristocracy.

Goguryeo Kingdom era tombs have for the most part been found in the North Korean city of Pyeongyang and in China's Jirin Province. The mural paintings produced inside of these tombs are quite elaborate in nature. More commonly known as the mural paintings of Goguryeo, these treasures were in 2004 included by UNESCO on its World Cultural Heritage List.

The people of Goguryeo created burial chambers by piling up stones; thereafter, graves were established by covering these burial chambers with earth. Each burial chamber was decorated with various paintings. For the people of Goguryeo, death represented a new start. In this regard, the life of the owner of the tomb during his passage in this world was vividly depicted within the tomb. More to the point, while aspects of everyday life were rendered on the walls, the elements belonging to the heavenly world, such as the sun, moon, and constellations, were painted on the ceiling. As such, the burial chamber was designed in a manner that resembled a small universe. These Goguryeo mural paintings belie highly-advanced architectural and artistic skills.

The mural paintings produced during the 4th-5th centuries depict many elements of everyday life. In addition, one also finds scenes depicting such mundane items as buildings, military marches, battles, hunting, dancing, kitchens, mills, stables, barns, and wells. However, the mural paintings produced during the 5th- 6th centuries feature the appearance of the sasindo or four guardian deities (blue dragon of the east, white tiger of the west, red phoenix of the south and black hyeonmu-an imaginary creature that is half-turtle-half-snake-of the north), as well as the lotus patterns reflecting the growing influence of Buddhism. Meanwhile, Taoist images, such as pictures of immortals and mountains, are featured in the mural paintings produced during the 6th-7th centuries.

The Goguryeo mural paintings represent a vivid depiction of the features of Goguryeo society. Through these paintings, which play the role of a kindly conveyer, one can come to better comprehend the thoughts, religions, culture, customs and traditions of the people of Goguryeo.

Contemplative Bodhisattva: The Thinker of Korea

The Banga sayusang, or Contemplative Bodhisattva, is a statue of a seated Maitreya Bodhisattva engaging in deep reflection over the salvation of the masses. Structures featuring the posture adopted by the Contemplative Bodhisattva first emerged in India. Originally involving renditions of the Buddha in his human form contemplating human life, this type of contemplative statue became very popular during the 5th- 6th centuries in China and the 6th- 7th centuries in Korea. The introduction of this type of contemplative statue in Korea was accompanied by the abandonment of the image of the Buddha in his princely human form in favor of the Maitreya Bodhisattva. Much like the Messiah in Christianity, the Maitreya is widely regarded in Buddhist scriptures as the eventual savior of the masses.

Koreans are particularly proud of two Contemplative Bodhisattvas crafted out of gilt-bronze that have come to be recognized as cultural properties ((National Treasures No. 83 and No. 78). The Contemplative Bodhisattva listed as National Treasure No. 83 not only vividly describes all the elements of a deep thinker, but also exhibits the essence of art. Simply put, it boasts a straightforward and plain and yet detailed and dignified beauty. The descriptions of the monotonous yet perfectly balanced body, and of the natural and elegant pleated cloth, expose the highly advanced nature of Korean sculpture during the 6th-7th centuries. In addition, the gentle smile spotted on this artistically perfect statue's lips is reminiscent of that of the Mona Lisa. The statue has received kudos from the world over and been proclaimed as a masterpiece of 6th - 7th century Oriental Buddhist art. For instance, French commentator Guy Sorman had the following to say about the Contemplative Bodhisattva, "I was attracted by the appearance of the statue which reminded me of Rodin's Thinker. This is a world-class cultural heritage equivalent to the Mona Lisa housed in the Louvre."

Korean-style contemplative statues were also conveyed to Japan. In fact, one of Japan's National Treasures, the Miroku Bosatsu, is very similar in nature to Korea's National Treasure No. 83: the Contemplative Bodhisattva. Given the fact that this was made of red pine, which was at that time only grown in Korea, many scholars have reached the conclusion that this wooden statue was in reality presented to Japan by Baekje Kingdom (18 BC - 660 AD) during the process through which the latter conveyed Confucianism, Buddhism, and architecture to Japan.

Geumdongbangasayusang, Gilt bronze Buddha sitting in meditation. A 90 cm high Buddha figure from the Baekje Dynasty(18 BC-660 AD) considered to be the best Buddha figure sculpture in Korea. National Treasure No. 83. The National Museum of Korea.

Seosan Mae Samjonbul:
The Smile of the Baekje Dynasty

The Seosan Mae Samjonbul (Three Buddhist Sculptures in Seosan) is the name given to three Buddhist sculptures which were engraved on a rock in Unsan-myeon, Seosan, Chungnam Province. Designated as National Treasure No. 84, the Seosan Mae Samjonbul was produced during the Baekje Kingdom era (18 BC - 660 AD). The sculptures consist of a Sakyamuni statue flanked by a standing Bodhisattva to the right and a Contemplative Bodhisattva to the left. The city of Seosan stood along the route which Baekje embarked on to trade with China. The presence of an international port in Seosan at that time has led many to conclude that these Buddhist sculptures were created as a means of praying for Baekje's prosperity and the safety of those who went to China to engage in trade.

Of the numerous rock-cut Buddhist sculptures found in Korea, the Seosan Mae Samjonbul has widely been hailed as the most outstanding masterpiece of the late Baekje era. The faces of the individuals in these Buddhist sculptures are animated by the presence of benevolent and delightful smiles. The warmhearted and romantic nature of the people of Baekje is rightly reflected in this masterpiece. The Sakyamuni statue stands 2.8m tall. Chubby-cheeked and endowed with friendly eyes adorned with long roundish eyebrows, the statue is believed to mirror the appearance of the people of Baekje. The pure benevolent smile found on this Buddhist sculpture has been referred to as the 'smile of Baekje'; it is a smile that belies the warmhearted spirit of the people of Baekje.

The smiles found on the Seosan Mae Samjonbul represent the extreme kindness that is only possible in an absolute being. Another unique feature of these statues is that their facial expressions change based on the direction of the sunlight. In his ‹A Record on the Exploration of Cultural Heritages› Yu Hong-jun described the smile of Baekje as follows:

"The smiles of these Buddhist sculptures look different in the morning than they do in the evening. The smile espoused in the evening is one of benevolent silence. Of all the seasons, the smile in autumn is by far the most beautiful. This most beautiful smile is created when the autumn sun sets over Seosan and darkness begins to fall."

The Seosan Mae Samjonbul is a masterpiece that allows all those who see it to focus on the spiritual world that is hinted at through the smiles on the sculptures rather than on the sculptures themselves. The techniques employed to create it belie a very advanced understanding of art. The wrinkled clothes worn by each of the statues leaves one feeling as if these garments could begin at any moment to flutter in the wind; moreover, their outstretched hands creates the sensation amongst visitors that these warm-hearted beings are reaching out to them.

Celadon (porcelain): The Essence of Ceramic

Ceramics are the pride(essence) of arts and crafts. Along with Chinese ceramics, Korean ceramics are the leaders in the history of ceramics. Korea has been producing ceramics since the 10th century. However Japan started producing ceramics in the 17th century by themselves while Europe started in the 18th century.

If ceramic pottery is the one made in low temperatures, porcelain are glazed with an enamel and made in high temperatures. In other words, procelain is a further developed form of ceramic. Porcelain was first produced in China. Around the 10th century, Goryeo Dynasty (918-1392) brought the porcelain technology from China and introduced it to their own country, during the 12th century and created works that shone in the world of ceramics. These works usually have a beautiful and radiating greenish color, and diverse and detailed concave or convex patterns. Also the artistic property and the balanced beauty of these ceramics reaches almost perfection. The Chinese people who developed these celadon considered these Goryeo ceramics the best in the world, and they wished to keep one in their homes.

The Goryeo celadon developed even further and evolved into the sanggamcheongja porcelain(inlaid celadon). This inlaid celadon is made with a technique developed solely by Goryeo ceramists who got the idea from metal crafting techniques such as the damascening that carves or inlays sanggam patterns with silver thread in the celadon. The appearance of the inlaid celadon brought a numerous variety of patterns compared to the Goryeo celadon. They carved countless patterns such as arabesque patterns dangchomun, lotus flower, peonies, chrysanthemums, phoenixes, cranes, clouds, bamboo trees and leaves. This is how they were able to produce ceramics with different atmosphere, impressions, tastes, mood and texture. Because of their unique qualities, these celadon made with the inlay technique receive special value and recognition in the history of world ceramics.

At the turn of the 14th century, the inlaid celadon slowly deteriorated and buncheongjagi (grayish stoneware) took its place. Along with the Goryeo inlaid celadon, buncheong wares are unique products that exist only in Korea. Bunchoeng wares are inlaid celadon painted with an additional coating of whitish soil. This is why buncheong wares usually give off a grayish color. Buncheong wares were at their peak from the late Goryeo period to the early Joseon period, after the 16th century. The colors, shapes and designs of the buncheong wares are for the masses. The patterns were modern and selected freely. Because the shape, patterns and colors of the bunchoeng wares were not showy they did not received much appeal or recognition from the common people. However they received a lot of attention from world ceramics experts and ceramic lovers.

Baekja(white porcelain): The Beauty of Restraint and the Esthetic of the Blank Space

The Baekja(white porcelain) coexisted with the buncho-eng wares during the 15th century and became the leading pottery of Korea in the 16th century. Baekja is a white-color celadon made with extremely fine white soil. There were several types of baekja including the sunsubaekja(pure white celadon) without any patterns or drawings on the surfaces, choenghwabaekja(jade white celadon), a celadon with glazed blue patterns, and cheolhwa baekja, patterns painted with wires. The baekja shows a static, simple, lonely and aristocratic beauty. The beauty of restraint and the esthetic of the blank space contained in the baekja is connected to Confucianism, the leading philosophical mentality of that period. While Goryeo Dynasty (918-1392) was a Buddhist nation, Joseon Dynasty (1392-1910) was a Confucian nation. Confucianism greatly influenced not only the world of politics, economy and society but also culture and the arts. Scholars and artists of the time thought highly of a righteous and humble life and this way of thinking was reflected en-tirely in their concept of aesthetics or beauty Consequently, Joseon Dynasty has simple and plain Indian ink paintings of natural landscapes instead of ostentatious color displays or the baekja with its modest and static beauty instead of the colorful Goryeo celadon. Also woodcrafts that maximized natural beauty reached its zenith during this period.

The leading philosophy of the Joseon period, which was to built a moral nation on Confucian thought, was reflected entirely in the art works.

The Joseon baekja made a critical contribution in opening the ceramic culture in Japan. Japan invaded Korea during the late 16th century, starting the fierce Hideyoshi Invasions (1592 - 1598) which lasted 7 years. During this war, Japan took around 1,000 Korean ceramic craftsmen by force. Up until then, Japan lacked the skills and techniques to make ceramics. These craftsmen opened the page of the Japanese ceramic history. Even today, Japanese people deify and look up to these potters and craftsmen.

Buncheong Ware: The Vessels of Freedom

Buncheong ware is a modernistic type of Korean stoneware whose heyday occurred during the 15th-16th centuries. The term buncheong refers to the process of coating white clay on cheongja (light-green hued ceramics). While the potters of Goryeo Dynasty (918 - 1392) had produced cheongja with the support of the ruling class, the collapse of the dynasty and subsequent rise of Joseon Dynasty (1392 - 1910) resulted in the main consumers of cheongja all but disappearing from the scene in one big swoop as the royal family of Goryeo was destroyed and the aristocracy was purged. In addition, scholars assumed the position of power previously held by monks within society. As a result, potters found themselves with little other choice but to scatter to all four corners of the land, where they consequently started to make the pieces of pottery demanded which the public needed as part of their everyday lives.

These new pieces were manufactured using methods that had previously been employed to manufacture cheongja. However, the cheongja which was produced in their new kilns were of an unclear rather than transparent green hue. This denouement was in large part the result of the fact that without the patronage of the ruling class, potters found themselves unable to purchase quality clay and glaze. Using their imaginations, these potters began to produce cheongja that were coated with a white slip. This was how buncheong ware emerged.

Buncheong wares were the first celadon vessels created under conditions in which the potters were effectively liberated from the support and demands of the ruling class. The strength that led to the creation of these buncheong wares can in this regard be perceived as having been rooted in this newly found freedom, as potters found themselves able to independently and freely reflect their own aesthetic sense and emotions in these wares. The abstractive patterns expressed in buncheong wares are in particular valued as an example of a modern sense of beauty.

The British potter and writer Bernard Howell Leach (1887 - 1979) once stated that, "Korean buncheong wares have already shown us the path which modern pottery should pursue." To this end, many Western art critics have advanced the notion that the Korean potters of the 15th century, who had already achieved modernity, had effectively reached a higher plain than modern Western counterparts such as Henri Matisse and Paul Klee.

©Leeum Museum

Maksabal: The Aesthetic Beauty of Simplicity

Maksabal (coarse stoneware) is a type of buncheong pottery (traditional Korean stoneware with a bluish-green tone) that first began to be used during the 15th century. While the cheongja (pale green hued porcelain) and baekja (white porcelain) were used by members of the royal family and aristocratic class, maksabal was employed by monks and commoners. While cheongja and baekja were produced by government-led kilns, maksabal was produced by private kilns in local areas. Moreover, unlike cheongja and baekja, maksabal was not used in conjunction with any special occasions. Although also used on occasion as a bowl in which rice, alcohol, or tea were stored, it was mainly used by monks. While 'mak' means roughly or recklessly, 'sabal' means a bowl made out of earth. As the name given to the bowl denotes, the maksabal was in fact coarse stoneware which was used by commoners during the Joseon Dynasty era (1392 - 1910).

All of this may create the impression that maksabal is a very ordinary form of ceramics. Nothing could be truer. Maksabal does not exude the sophistication displayed by cheongja or the sense of dignity exhibited by baekja. It is a simple, unsophisticated, and natural form of ceramics. There is an old Korean saying that, "It which contains the least contains the most." In this regard, maksabal can be construed as a perfect example of the veracity of this saying. As such, maksabal, which is neither excessive nor lacking in anything, incorporates the tenets of the doctrine of the mean. Herein lies the greatness and attraction of maksabal.

Maksabal began to make their way into to Japan during the 16th century. As Japan did not possess any techniques to produce ceramics and pottery of their own, they imported them from Joseon Dynasty. While these maksabal were used as rice bowls in Joseon Dynasty, they became tea receptacles in Japan. They were especially popular amongst Japanese samurais and monks, who referred to maksabal as Ido Dawan.

Not having any real containers in which to drink tea of their own, maksabal came to hold a special place in the hearts of the Japanese as well. They regarded maksabal as extremely valuable items and even as family treasures. Maksabal became perceived by the Japanese people as a symbol of wealth, and continues to be held in high esteem to this day. About 200 pieces of maksabal were produced in Japan during the 16th century. Of these, the maksabal housed in the Daitoku-Ji Temple in Kyoto has been designated as a national treasure by the Japanese government. While three other pieces have also been designated as national treasures, another twenty have received the title of important cultural properties.

Maksabal (coarse stoneware) is a type of buncheong pottery (traditional Korean stoneware with a bluish-green tone) that first began to be used during the 15th century. While 'mak' means roughly or recklessly, 'sabal' means a bowl made out of earth.

Pungmulgut: Where Work and Play Collide

Pungmulgut refers to a communal form of recreation popular in Korean agrarian society. Integrating musical performances, dancing, singing, and dramatic elements, the pungmulgut has widely been regarded as mirroring the lifestyle of the Korean minjung (people). More to the point, the pungmulgut incorporates the smell of the earth, hard labor, and wishes of the Korean people. These events also reflected the strong will of the common people to live dignified lives despite the presence of numerous natural disasters and rampant oppression on the part of the ruling class.

The kkangwari (small gong), jing (round metal gong), janggu (hourglass-shaped drum), and buk (drum) are the main musical instruments used in conjunction with the pungmulgut. These instruments are meant to represent the sounds of nature. While the kkangwari, which achieves the highest tone, is meant to describe thunder, the janggu exudes a joyful sound that is reminiscent of rain. For their part, the buk, which forms the backbone of the pungmulgut, represents clouds, while the jing, which embraces the sounds of other musical instruments and emits a long lingering sound, represents the wind. The sounds created by these instruments were more than the simple sounds of instruments; they were the voices of Koreans attempting to convey the contents of their hearts and minds to the heavens.

The origin of pungmulgut can be traced back to rituals to the heavens conducted during the prehistoric era. The pungmulgut emerged once these rituals to the heavens became more formal, and the musical instruments used to implement them more advanced. However, it was during the Joseon Dynasty era (1392-1910) that the pungmulgut came to take on today's appearance. The farmers of Joseon possessed a tradition known as dure which revolved around the men coming together to help others within their communities. Farmers attempted to soothe the bumps and bruises incurred during their grueling work process by listening to music performed using these instruments. Over time, this practice came to be called 'dure pungmul'. This dure pungmul became more organized as the dure tradition took root, eventually becoming the pungmulgut.

The pungmulgut went into rapid decline during the Japanese colonial era (1910 - 1945). As part of their efforts to eradicate the Korean culture and communal spirit, the Japanese imperialists prohibited the holding of pungmulgut. During this period, the only reason for which the playing of pungmul was permitted was for agricultural promotion purposes. This resulted in pungmulgut being downgraded to simple farmers' music, or 'nongak', within the Korean psyche.

It was during the 1970s that the revival of the pungmulgut began in earnest within Korean society. The advent of labor strife caused by industrialization, and university students joining of the democratization movement had the effect of resulting in a resurgence of the pungmulgut that had traditionally served as a form of recreation amongst the minjung. It was during this period that the composition of the pungmulgut was transformed as stage-based percussion performances known as 'samul nori' became increasingly more common. Samul is a term used to collectively refer to the four instruments known individually as kkangwari (small gong), jing (round metal gong), jang-gu (hourglass-shaped drum), and buk (drum).

The pungmulgut has the power to bring people together and allow them to share in joyful moments with one another. This community-oriented sense of oneness is rooted in the life and dreams of the Korean minjung (people).

Talchum: A Performance in which the Audience Takes Part

Talchum is a traditional mask dance performance which was used by commoners as a means of criticizing the ruling class and to satire social contradictions. Talchum shares certain similarities with the mask performances found in other countries, in that, it is a form of performance or dance which is conducted while wearing masks. However, it exhibits differences in terms of the structure of the performance. Thus, while mask performances in other countries are structured in such a manner that the performers and audience are clearly separated from one another, talchum performances are designed to facilitate communication between the performers and spectators. This is because talchum is an open-air event held in a circular-shaped yard in which the performers and spectators freely interact with one another.

Talchum, a Korean traditional folk performance which has its origins in the Three Kingdoms Era (57 BC - 660 AD), developed greatly during the Joseon dynasty. Up until the 1970s, this art form was known simply as a masked performance. However, the democratization movement led by university students in the 1980s used such masked performances, which featured aspects of populism, social critique, satire and humor, as one of the tools with which to achieve democratization. Using these masked performances, the students brought to light and lampooned the tyranny and oppression of the ruling class, as well as the inherent social contradic-

tions. Thereafter, such masked performances began to be called talchum.

One does not need to be a specialized performer to take part in talchum. Rather, anybody can take part in this particular art form. In addition, unlike other types of performances, the fact that the performers are free to interact with the spectators in a circular yard makes it such that talchum is an art form which features a high degree of audience participation. As such, these university students were able to express their intentions to audiences that gathered in these round courtyards through the dances, songs, and acting which they undertook as part of their talchum performances.

While the center of the courtyard serves as the stage, the surroundings become the auditorium. As mentioned above, the spectators can actively participate in talchum performances. The audience sitting around the stage is expected to help the performers maintain the rhythm, and may be called on to play a small role in the performance at a moment's notice. As such, the audience acts as both a spectator and a participant in the talchum.

Talchum is a comprehensive performance that combines dancing, singing, and narration. The attractiveness of talchum lies in its candor. As it is performed while wearing masks, spectators are able to feel a sense of openness and vivacity that can hardly be experienced in other genres. People's personalities are instantly altered the moment they put on a mask, which in this case acts as a tool which allows them to vividly express the sadness and rancor which festers in their hearts. A mask in itself is nothing more than a piece of plastic art. However, talchum allows a mask to develop its own spirit and the ability to move people's hearts and minds.

Pansori: Korean Opera

Pansori is a Korean traditional performing art in which one singer (changja or sorikkun) tells a dramatic story while a drummer (gosu) plays on in the background. Although outwardly similar to Western-style opera, pansori stands out because of the fact that it features only one singer conveying stories amidst various rhythms emanating from a drummer.

As the changja must play all the characters that appear in a story, she or he must have the ability to carry out vocals in various octaves. Meanwhile, the gosu, or drummer, must possess the ability to always choose the appropriate rhythm at the right time. As such, the gosu can make or break a pansori performance.

Viewed from the outside, pansori appears to be a simple form of performance art which does not require any special techniques. However, the singer and drummer must in fact master various techniques such as that of aniri, sori, ballim, and chuimsae. Aniri refers to a break in the music during which time the performer engages in narration. Meanwhile, sori, which is also called chang, refers to musical expressions through sounds and rhythms and ballim refers to body gestures used to help convey the story to the audience.

Chuimsae are interjections such as eolssigu(yippee!), jota(that's good!), and geureochi(ok!) which are meant to serve as encouragement. While the aniri, sori, and ballim are carried out by the singer (changja), the chuimsae is conducted by the drummer (gosu) to inspire the singer and excite the audience. The audience may also join the gosu in engaging in chuimsae. The joining in of the audience is believed to heighten the value of the performance. Pansori is thus a style of performance in which the stage, singer, drummer, and audience becomes are joyously harmonized with one another.

Pansori is a comprehensive art form which combines literary, musical, and dramatic elements. It tells about life through words, creates musical beauty through sound, and uses gestures to get at the truth.

Pansori first emerged during the 18th century. While 12 works are known to have originally existed, only five now remain (Chunhyangga, Heungbuga, Sugungga, Jeokbyeokga, and Simcheongga). In this regard, while the Chunhyangga is a story which depicts the human will to move beyond the fetters of social class, the Sugungga is one in which the contradictions of feudal society and the solutions to these contradictions are clearly expressed. Meanwhile, the Heungbuga deals with the issue of poverty and wealth. Although pansori works would appear on the surface to be based on idealism, they in fact incorporate and reflect the reality of the minjung (people). For instance, they include their criticism of social inequality and fallacies.

Pansori is as such a performing art that encompasses the lives of everyone from the commoner to the yangban(the nobility).

Pansori is filled with humor and jokes. While its rhythmic lilts create a sense of excitement, the metaphors employed fill the audience's minds with vivid images.

The beautiful sounds of pansori have become emblematic of Korea. In this regard, UNESCO listed pansori on the list of Masterpiece of the Oral and Intangible Heritage of Humanity in November 2003.

Arirang: Song of Korean Souls

Arirang is a Korean folk song that features a long oral tradition. While every Korean can sing Arirang, it is not known who created this song or when it first started to be sung. The first documented version of the Arirang song is the Jeongseon Arirang, so-named because it was created in the village of Jeongseon in Gangwon-Do Province around 600 AD. Interestingly, versions of the Arirang song featuring rhythms and words unique to each area began to appear after 600. These include the Milyang Arirang, Gangwondo Arirang, and Jindo Arirang. The version of Arirang that is now most beloved by Koreans, known as the Bonjo Arirang, was first composed at the end of the 19th century. Based on the Jeongseon Arirang, this version has also been referred to as the New Arirang.

While the exact meaning of the term 'Arirang' has never been transmitted, Koreans have often labeled a hill or mountain that is difficult to surmount as an 'arirang gogae'. With this in mind, many have reached the conclusion that the song Arirang is a piece that is laden with the sentiment of han (resentment).

Arirang involves the repetitive singing of the refrain and verses. The refrain goes as follows:
The verses are at once beautiful and sad.

Refrain
Arirang, Arirang, Arariyo...
Arirang gogaero neomeoganda.
(Arirang, Arirang, Arariyo,
Arirang Pass is the long road you go.)

Arirang has three verses. They are listed below:

Verse 1
Nareul beorigo gasineun nimeun
Simnido motgaseo balbyeongnanda
(Dear who abandoned me here
Will not walk even ten-li (4km) before his/her feet hurt.)

Verse 2
Cheongcheonghaneuren byeoldo manko
Urine gaseumen kkumdo manta
(Just as there are many stars in the clear sky,
There are also many dreams in our heart.)

Verse 3

Jeogi jeo sani Baekdusaniraji
Dongji seotdaredo kkonman pinda
(There, over there that mountain is Baekdu Mountain,
Where, even in the middle of winter days, flowers bloom.)

For a long period of time, Arirang was employed as a song of protest against the ruling class, or as a means of exhibiting one's love for nature and humanity. During the Japanese colonial era (1910 - 1945), Koreans sang Arirang as a means of consoling their souls and stoking the sense of resentment they felt at having lost their sovereignty. Meanwhile, during the Korean War (1950 - 53), Arirang became a song sung by those who dreamt of peace. However, Arirang is no longer regarded as a sad song. Koreans now sing Arirang when they feel happy or joyful. In fact, Arirang was even sung by fans to express their support for the home side during the 2002 Korea-Japan World Cup.

In addition, the New York Philharmonic's performance of Arirang during its very first concert ever staged in Pyeongyang in February 2008 left an indelible mark on all of those who heard it. UNESCO established an 'Arirang Award' in 2001. This award is bestowed upon individuals who have made a positive contribution to preserving and developing mankind's various cultural heritages. Needless to say, this is an award which Koreans are especially proud of.

Geomungo:
The Essence of Korean Musical Instruments

Geomungo is a traditional Korean string instrument. There are many traditional Korean paintings and poems which contain images of the geomungo. This wondrous instrument has a tonal quality that tugs at one's heart and embeds the lyrical emotions of all Koreans. In short, the national sentiment of Koreans is expressed through this geomungo. In his poem entitled 'Geomungo' the poet Kim Yeong-nang (1903-1950) stated that his voice or lamentations could never envelop the deep range of emotions which he and his people experienced during the Japanese colonial era (1910-1945) like the geomungo could.

According to the *Samguksagi* (Chronicles of the Three Kingdoms), the geomungo was created by Prime Minister Wang San-ak of the Goguryeo Kingdom (37 BC - 688 AD) while the latter attempted to remodel the seven-stringed harp that had been imported from China's Jin dynasty. As a black crane began to dance around when Wang San-ak played the geomungo, the instrument also came to be called a hyun-hakgeum (black crane zither). The origins of the geomungo are vividly depicted in the mural paintings of Goguryeo produced during the 5th -6th century.

It was during the Joseon Dynysty era (1392-1910) that the geomungo became the symbol of Korean string instruments. Geomungo performances were especially beloved by the members of the yangban (the nobility) class, who regarded the ability to perform the geomungo as one of the virtues which the seonbi should possess. The seonbi (literati) played the geomungo as part of their efforts at self-cultivation.

While the front plate of the instrument is made of paulownia wood, the back one is crafted out of hard chestnut wood. The six strings, which are made of twisted silk, are passed through its back plate and into the hollow body. It is said that in order to achieve the profound type of sounds which the instrument is capable of, the geomungo should only be performed by those with a clean mind. In this regards, people have claimed that it should not be performed in a heavy wind or rain, when one has to meet people with clouded minds, when one is not wearing proper clothing, when one is on the street, or when one does not have any appropriate place to seat. This means that the profound sound can only be created when one empties and purifies his mind. Geomungo is the musical instrument that is played with the soul.

Daegeum:
Summoning Koreans' Souls

Although Koreans are a dynamic people, a profound sense of sadness also animates their hearts. This is a sadness that has become internalized over the 5,000-year history of the nation. Koreans have developed many means to express and soothe this sadness, including festivals, music, work, and games. The musical instrument known as the daegeum (large bamboo transverse flute) has stood next to Koreans every step of the way on this quest to soothe this sadness. Two different kinds of daegeum exist: the jeongak daegeum and the sanjo daegeum. More to the point, while the jeongak daegeum was used to perform palace music, the sanjo daegeum was used to play folk music.

Daegeum has long held an important status within Korean traditional music. This is because the daegeum plays the main role during a concert. In addition, its relatively stable

Painting in which a performer can be seen playing the daegeum on the left side. Kim Hongdo's painting of a dancing boy(18c). Treasure No. 527, The National Museum of Korea.

musical pitch results in it becoming the standard against which other musical instruments are adjusted. The daegeum's ability to produce various sounds, ranging from a soft, profound sound to a thrillingly upbeat one, it is also used to perform solo recitals.

The expression of Koreans' sadness is not the only purpose for which the daegeum has been used. In this regard, the *Samgukyusa* (Legends and History of the Three Kingdoms of Ancient Korea) and *Samguksagi* (Chronicles of the Three Kingdoms) contains records relating to a legendary flute known as the Manpasikjeok which existed during the reign of King Sinmun (r. 681-692) of Silla Kingdom. This flute, which was made of bamboo, is credited with such miracles as having driven away enemies, removed epidemic diseases, and calmed the waves. Regarded as a flute which protected the country whenever a crisis engulfed the nation, it was subsequently designated as a national treasure.

The daegeum is a musical instrument that at once consoles the sadness of Koreans while also awakening their souls. The sound of the daegeum instantly reminds Koreans of who they are.

Chunhyangjeon: Korea's Love Story

Chunhyangjeon is a classic Korean novel of romance that has been compared by some to the story of Romeo and Juliette. The story revolves around two starry-eyed lovers: Chunhyang, the daughter of a former kisaeng (Korean female entertainer), and Lee Mong-nyong, the son of the governor of the city of Namwon in Jeonbuk Province. The actual author of this story remains unknown. This is because *Chunhyangjeon* is a pansori-based novel. Pansori-based novels involve traditional tales which first became the subject of pansori (Korean traditional performing art) and were then turned into novels. Thus, because *Chunhyangjeon* was based on a traditional tale which had been orally conveyed, there is no way of ascertaining its actual author.

Chunhyangjeon is in many ways the amalgamation of various tales. In fact, it constitutes the combination of stories such as those of a woman who kept her chastity, of valiant efforts to protect the weak from the tyranny of those with power, of the consolation provided to the spirits of those who died unfairly, of love, and of a government official trying to steal the wife of a commoner. Chunhyang and Mongnyong are two star-crossed lovers who fall in love and get married without telling their parents about it. However, Mongnyong is forced to go back to Hanyang (presently Seoul) when his father's tenure as the governor of Namwon comes to an end. Mongnyong promises his young bride that he will return for her after having passed the civil official examination (gwageo). Meanwhile, a new governor is appointed in Namwon. Soon Chunhyang finds herself summoned to entertain the new governor. However, Chunhyang refuses to do on the grounds that she is in fact a married woman. For her refusal, she is tortured and thrown into prison. One day, a beggarly-looking Mongnyong shows up at the prison where Chunhyang is incarcerated. Although scheduled to be executed on the new governor's birthday, Chunhyang finds herself more worried about Mongnyong's ratty appearance and her inability to do anything for him. Soon, the new governor's birthday arrives and a large party is held to commemorate the event. However, before Chunhyang can be executed, a secret royal inspector steps forward to save her. This secret royal inspector is revealed to be none other than Mongnyong. Having saved his beloved from the jaws of death, Mongnyong and Chunhyang go on to live a happy life as husband and wife.

This story became a classic of Korean literature in large part because Chunhyang's drive to keep her love alive despite the presence of numerous obstacles and difficulties is one which resonates with Koreans. Some have concluded that given the backdrop against which this story unfolds, the novel was in all likelihood created during the late Joseon (17th - 18th century) era. This period was one in which a rigid social class system rooted in a feudal structure held sway. As such, this story of requited love between the daughter of a low-born kisaeng and the son of a yangban (the nobility) filled the hearts of people with a sense of freedom and hope for the future.

There are currently more than 120 different versions of the *Chunhyangjeon*. This is because the original tale of the *Chunhyangjeon* has been adjusted or updated to reflect the circumstances of a particular period. The 20th century has seen has this classic tale be recreated as a changgeuk (traditional Korean opera), opera, film, and drama, all of which have filled the hearts of Koreans with hopes that their dreams will also be fulfilled.

100 Cultural Symbols of Korea

First Edition **September 10, 2008**

Authors **Yoo Myeong-jong, Lee Ji-hye**
Photographer **Jeon Sung-young**
Translators **You Young-ki and Michael Bujold**
Designer **Mun Soo-min**
Publisher **Yoo Myeong-jong**
Published by **Discovery media**

Registration Number **22-2486** | Registration Date **February 11, 2004**
431, King's Garden Office hotel 3rd Complex, 72, Naesoo-dong, Jongno-gu, Seoul, Korea
Tel **82-2-587-5558** | Fax **82-2-588-5558**

Printed in Korea

ISBN 978-89-956091-6-3 03900

About the authors

Yoo Myeong-jong is a poet and cultural critic who majored in Korean language & literature at Korea University. His professional career has included stints as a reporter for Monthly *Literature & Thought*, *Roots and Wings*, and Koreana. He also served as the editor-in-chief of Toyota Korea's *Lexus Magazine*, as well as for *Morning Calm*, Korean Air's in-flight magazine. Mr. Yoo has contributed numerous essays on topics such as photography, art, architecture and Korean culture to various magazines. In addition to being the co-author of the poetry compilation *My Hearts Soars Whenever I Hear Your Voice*, he has also published books such as *The Discovery of Korea*, *The Discovery of Seoul*, and *Images of Korea*.

Lee Ji-hye is a poet and a freelance writer who graduated from Hanyang University. The publication in 1989 of one of her poems in the winter issue of World Literature (segyeui munhak) marked her official entrance into literary circles. From the mid-1990s onwards, Ms. Lee began to regularly contribute photo essays and articles in magazines such as Toyota Korea's *Lexus Magazine*, Ssangyong's *Yeouiju*, and *Morning Calm*, Korean Air's in-flight magazine. She has also contributed essay pieces and photo essays on the subject of Korean cultural properties of Korea to various magazines, including *Love of Korea's Cultural Heritage* published by the Cultural Heritage Administration of Korea.

Jeon Sung-young is a documentary photographer who majored in photography at Shingu College. Since the mid-1990s, he has devoted himself to travelling throughout Northeast China, the Korean peninsula, and Japan in order to capture images of ancient Korean relics with his camera. He has contributed historical documentary photographs to various magazines, including *Morning Calm* Korean Air's in-flight magazine. He also served as the Third President of the Korea Publishing Photographer Society, and was actively involved with the Baekje Institute in his capacity as a board member. Mr. Jeon is the author of the book, *Dreams of Goguryeo at the Thousand League Wall*.

Korea Foundation
한국국제교류재단
The Korea Foundation has provided financial assistance for the undertaking of this publication project.